Actors and the Art of Performance

Performance Philosophy

Series Editors:
Laura Cull Ó Maoilearca (University of Surrey, UK)
Alice Lagaay (Zeppelin University, Friedrichshafen, Germany)
Freddie Rokem (Tel Aviv University, Israel)

Performance Philosophy is an emerging interdisciplinary field of thought, creative practice and scholarship. The *Performance Philosophy* book series comprises monographs and essay collections addressing the relationship between performance and philosophy within a broad range of philosophical traditions and performance practices, including drama, theatre, performance arts, dance, art and music. The series also includes studies of the performative aspects of life and, indeed, philosophy itself. As such, the series addresses the philosophy of performance as well as performance-as-philosophy and philosophy-as-performance.

Editorial Advisory Board:
Emmanuel Alloa (University of St. Gallen, Switzerland), Lydia Goehr (Columbia University, USA), James R. Hamilton (Kansas State University, USA), Bojana Kunst (Justus-Liebig University Giessen, Germany), Nikolaus Müller-Schöll (Goethe University Frankfurt am Main, Germany), Martin Puchner (Harvard University, USA), Alan Read (King's College London, UK)

Titles include:

Laura Cull & Alice Lagaay (*eds*)
ENCOUNTERS IN PERFORMANCE PHILOSOPHY (*2014*)

Broderick Chow & Alex Mangold (*eds*)
ŽIŽEK AND PERFORMANCE (*2014*)

Will Daddario & Karoline Gritzner (*eds*)
ADORNO AND PERFORMANCE (*2014*)

Stuart Grant, Jodie McNeilly & Maeva Veerapen (*eds*)
PERFORMANCE AND TEMPORALISATION (*2014*)

Bojana Cvejic (*author*)
CHOREOGRAPHING PROBLEMS
Expressive Concepts in European Contemporary Dance and Performance (*2015*)

Forthcoming titles:

Mischa Twitchin (*author*)
THE THEATRE OF DEATH
The Uncanny in Mimesis (*2016*)

Published in association with the research network
Performance Philosophy www.performancephilosophy.ning.com

PERFORMANCE PHILOSOPHY

palgrave▶pivot

Actors and the Art of Performance: Under Exposure

Susanne Valerie

Professor, University of Music and Performing Arts, Vienna, Austria

Translated from the German by
Laura Radosh with Alice Lagaay

 Except where otherwise noted, this work is licensed under a Creative Commons Attribution 4.0 International License. To view a copy of this license, visit https://creativecommons.org/version4

Published with the support of the Austrian Science Fund (FWF): PUB 357-Z24. Research results from Austrian Science Fund (FWF) [TRP12-G21].

ACTORS AND THE ART OF PERFORMANCE: UNDER EXPOSURE
Copyright © Susanne Valerie, 2016
Translation © Laura Radosh and Alice Lagaay

All rights reserved.

Open access:

 This work is licensed under a Creative Commons Attribution 4.0 International License. The images or other third party material in this article are included in the work's Creative Commons license, unless indicated otherwise in the credit line; if the material is not included under the Creative Commons license, users will need to obtain permission from the license holder to reproduce the material. To view a copy of this license, visit http://creativecommons.org/licenses/by/4.0/

First published 2016 by
PALGRAVE MACMILLAN

The author has asserted her right to be identified as the author of this work in accordance with the Copyright, Designs and Patents Act 1988.

Palgrave Macmillan in the UK is an imprint of Macmillan Publishers Limited, registered in England, company number 785998, of Houndmills, Basingstoke, Hampshire RG21 6XS.

Palgrave Macmillan in the US is a division of Nature America, Inc., One New York Plaza, Suite 4500 New York, NY 10004–1562.

Palgrave Macmillan is the global academic imprint of the above companies and has companies and representatives throughout the world.

Hardback ISBN: 978–1–137–59633–8
E-PUB ISBN: 978–1–137–59635–2
E-PDF ISBN: 978–1–137–59634–5
DOI: 10.1057/9781137596345

Distribution in the UK, Europe and the rest of the world is by Palgrave Macmillan®, a division of Macmillan Publishers Limited, registered in England, company number 785998, of Houndmills, Basingstoke, Hampshire RG21 6XS.

Library of Congress Cataloging-in-Publication Data is available from the Library of Congress

A catalogue record for this book is available from the Library of Congress

A catalogue record for the book is available from the British Library

▶ *Schauspieler außer sich: Exponiertheit und performative Kunst. Eine feminine Recherche*, Susanne Valerie Granzer, Originally published in German in 2011 Copyright of the first edition: transcript Verlag, Bielefield, Germany.

> Why could the world
> *which is of any concern to us* –
> not be a fiction?[1]
>
> We are simply fools of the theater![2]

---

1. Friedrich Nietzsche, *Beyond Good and Evil*, trans. R.J. Hollingdale (London: Penguin, 1990), 66.
2. Susanne Granzer, "Being on Stage," in *Ereignis Denken*, Arno Böhler and Susanne Granzer (eds) (Vienna: Passagen Verlag 2009), 78.

To my husband, Arno – my joy

Contents

Acknowledgments	x
About the Author	xi
Nous Pathetikos	**1**
Why do you want to be an actor?	2

Part I Hits

1	**Auditorium X**	**5**
	Double stalemate	6
	Turning point, peripeteia	10
	Turn around	12
	i, mine	14
2	**Speculations**	**15**
	Actors' fears	16
	Crying	18
	Child's play	22
	Exposed	23
	With-out me	30
3	**Black Out**	**34**
	First time at the theater	35

Part II Experts in Being?

4	**The Actor: A Creature of Fable**	**41**
	Why do you want to be an actor?	42
5	**The Causa Corpora**	**48**
	The kiss of Olympia	49

	Machine against man	50
	The actor's trump card	52
6	The Gift of Acting	58
	Skipping	59
	Prejudice	61
	Subject-based thinking versus stage experience	64
	Master and servant	67
	Bodies on stage	74
	Innocence of becoming	76
	Language and speaking	79
	Digesting speech	81
	Counterwords	83
	The Other, the others	84
	Affect versus thought	87
	Thinking and acting	91
	Repetition	93
7	The Gift of Death	103
	Tu es mort	104
	Theater as a symbolic death	105
	Point of no return	109
	Felicity – a salto mortale	111
	Our friend Touchstone	115
8	Finale and Punctum	119
	Why do you want to be an actor?	120

Acknowledgments

Special thanks are due to the Austrian Science Fund (FWF) for generously funding the translation of this book, which was originally written as part of the FWF research project "Generating Bodies. Corporeal Performance" (TRP 12-G21/2010–2013). I am currently undertaking research within the framework of the follow-up PEEK project, "Artist Philosophers – Philosophy as Arts-Based-Research" (AR 275-G21/2014–2017). I would like to take this opportunity to express my gratitude to the philosopher Arno Böhler, the instigator and director of both these FWF research projects.

My heartfelt thanks go to Laura Radosh, who, with careful attentiveness to the polyphonic layers of my book, has provided an English translation with a skill and sensitivity that do justice to the various philosophic and artistic references at play. This was surely no small feat. The translation was commissioned and supervised throughout by Alice Lagaay, without whom this book would not be available to English readers now. Alice's philosophic and multilingual competence, her dedication, and the infectious enthusiasm of her spirit made working on this project a real pleasure, for which I am immensely grateful to her.

About the Author

Susanne Valerie Granzer. Professor and actress. Starring roles at National State Theatres in Europe (Vienna, Basel, Düsseldorf, Frankfurt, and Berlin). Parallel to her professional work as an actress, she studied Philosophy at the Goethe-University Frankfurt and the University of Vienna and received her PhD in 1995. In 1988, she received a call for a full professorship in the central artistic subject "Acting" at the University of Music and Performing Arts, Vienna, Max Reinhardt Seminar. Together with the Austrian philosopher Arno Boehler, she founded in 1997 the Viennese art factory GRENZ-film and in 2005 the philosophy festival "Philosophy on Stage" based on their artistic research. Website: http://personal.mdw.ac.at/granzer/wp/.

OPEN

Nous Pathetikos

Abstract: Actors and the Art of Performance *opens with a cascade of contradictory motives for becoming an actor. These motives converge in the particular fascination of theater, in which ethics are realized in the aesthetic.*

Valerie, Susanne. *Actors and the Art of Performance: Under Exposure.* Basingstoke: Palgrave Macmillan, 2016. DOI: 10.1057/9781137596345.0004.

Why do you want to be an actor?

This is a played-out, bland question, overused and much abused, a colorless, powerless, boring question of no worth. It is heard too often, posed too often, answered too often. Full of inescapable, preprogrammed clichés, not even productive stuttering provides a way out. It is a question best left unasked. Such is the crux of the matter.

Or is it not an indispensable, essential, exciting question? Is it not a question that begs to be asked again and again, a disturbing, disquieting question, one that turns up the heat, knows no answer and has many answers, none of which suffice, and yet which despite it all, naive or not, embarrassing or not, promising or not, sprout up like polyphonous weeds.

Why? For the love of playing the play. Because it is fun. Because it is thrilling, or for the love of the spectacle, for the love of mimicry, out of obsession. Because it just took hold of me. Out of curiosity. To play great roles, leading roles: Hamlet, Don Carlos, Antigone, Lady Bracknell. Not Emilia, but evil Iago, and then perhaps demented King Lear. Or Joan of Arc? Oh, definitely, and then wild Medea. To play the entire canon of the classics and, of course, what is in vogue now too. To be famous, to become a star. To change the world, not just interpret it. To give people something out of a passion for fantasy, for the imaginary, for imagination. For the love of abundance. For the love of lies, not those that make your nose grow longer, but the ones that play with truth. Out of a fascination for masquerade, a fascination for transformation, both of which are irresistible. To be someone else, to create another being, to be many. For it all never to end. To be free. To fly. Openness immemorial. Openness without ideologies or theologies, openness as possibility – as the vacant space within us, kept open not out of destructiveness, but as a form of affirmation.

"To make believe," was the answer given by Kate Falk from the New York Wooster Group, when asked why she acts in the theater.[1]

---

1 "Theater morgen, Gespräche über die Kunst im Global Village." *Treffpunkt Kultur* ORF. Production: GRENZ-film (production team Arno Böhler and Susanne Granzer), ORF, 1998. All translations by Laura Radosh unless stated otherwise.

Why? To remain true to that which disconcerts, to not become jaded. To not grovel, not conform. To keep your eye on the prize, even if it is blinding. No boorish posing whatever the form – neither the dramatic, nor the postdramatic kind. No getting all worked up about what you always knew. No matter how old or how young you are, not to adhere to any rules that cannot be thrown overboard. To hold disdain for conventionalists and conformists, whether their comfort zone is on the right or on the left, and to hold disdain for the poison of resentment and for every self-appointed lord, no matter what his kingdom. To maintain a deep-seated aversion to standardized utilitarianism. To resist ogling the acceptable. To oppose the dictatorship of the highest possible number. To be different and live differently. To maximize, not minimize, risk. To stand against the times, to be untimely, whatever that might mean. And above all to be neither a hamster in a wheel nor an administrator of being, nor a careerist, nor a singer of the swan song of a late culture.

Maybe to become a fabled creature of truth?

Calm down. Get a grip on yourself.

Why?

As G.W.F. Hegel says in the famous preface to the *Phenomenology of Spirit*, "The True is...the Bacchanalian revel in which no member is not drunk."[2]

---

2   G.W.F. Hegel, *Phenomenology of Spirit*, trans. A.V. Miller (Oxford: Oxford University Press, 1977), 27.

OPEN

Part I
Hits

OPEN

1
Auditorium X

Abstract: *For weeks, a young acting student has been struggling unsuccessfully with a monologue from Schiller's The Maid of Orleans. Everyone is wondering whether to end rehearsals. It seems only a question of time. But then, unexpectedly, a change occurs. She finally begins to play the role well. It is a pleasure to watch. And then, just as things are looking good, there is a second shift. The student breaks into tears and no longer wants to act. What has happened?*

Valerie, Susanne. *Actors and the Art of Performance: Under Exposure.* Basingstoke: Palgrave Macmillan, 2016.
DOI: 10.1057/9781137596345.0006.

Double stalemate

Hannah J., a drama student, is struggling with one of the long monologues in Friedrich Schiller's romantic tragedy, *The Maid of Orleans*. There is no way to sweeten the experience. The rehearsal is grueling for everyone involved, and not for the first time. Each attempt at the play is polished and conventional. It is full of clichés, caught up in itself, locked into itself. Working on the play is like running a treadmill; it is not going anywhere. A stalemate. A bane.

Admittedly, the text is difficult, awkward. The language and the piece itself have an unfamiliar feel. They raise more than one aesthetic and thematic question. Nowadays, other theatrical forms have led to a radical caesura in classical drama. Even Friedrich Nietzsche's the *Twilight of the Idols* attacked Schiller as "the Moral-Trumpeter of Säckingen."[1] The power of Logos has been dislodged by the logic of the fragment.

No matter how you look at it – is it any wonder that in the late modern era a young actor finds it hard to connect to a figure like Joan of Arc? That she struggles with sentences such as:

Who? I? I hold the image of
A man in this pure heart of mine?
This heart can pulse with earthly love,
That Heaven fills with light divine?
I, who am my country's savior,
Almighty God's own warrior,
I for my country's foe dare yearn?
Do I dare to the chaste sun turn
And will not shame annihilate me?[2]

How can an actor today approach a text like this? How can she play and *embody* this text on stage? How can she speak this text by "heart"? How does Schiller's language feel 200 years later? How does it taste, what does

---

[1] Friedrich Nietzsche, *Twilight of the Idols*, trans. R.J. Hollingdale (London: Penguin Books, 1990), 78. Unless noted otherwise, this is the translation of *Twilight of the Idols* cited.

[2] Friedrich Schiller, *Maid of Orleans*, trans. Charles E. Passage (New York: Frederick Unger Publishing, 1967), Act IV, Scene I, 87.

it transport, what can we still read, what can we not read, what can we play, what can we not play? Ergo. How can an actor today speak Schiller's words without losing *tête, ventre et queue* (head, stomach and tail),[3] to cite Jean-Luc Nancy.

Do the roots of Hannah J.'s difficulties therefore lie in Schiller's classical dramatic text, which has long given up its place in the canon of theater? Would it be better to stage the play without its dramatis personae and their traditional dialogues, perhaps in a plane of language[4] or as an adaptation of a novel, allowing the creation of new free texts and forms? Does the text make her feel compelled to fulfill the traditional expectation of an "authentic" psychological interpretation? Does it make her feel bound to reproduce an illusion even when there is no need for this kind of portrayal? Or is she just insecure, overwhelmed by the pros and cons of all the different ways contemporary theater can deal with thematic and aesthetic problems? Are they the source of the intractable situation she is now stuck in?

No. Instinctively you shake your head. No, the trouble Hannah J. is having could arise in all theatrical forms. Her difficulties have another feel and even another smell.

The fact is, the girl is struggling on stage. She cannot find a way into the text, the role, the situation, or the emotions. Her words are made of paper, her body of clay. There is no flow, no groove, no *play*. Everything still feels constructed, fabricated, empty. It stumbles, falters, stagnates, and gets stuck. But why?

---

3 "Platon veut que discours ait le corps bien constitué d'un grand animal, avec tête, ventre et queue. C'est pourquoi nous autres, bons et vieux platoniciens, nous savons et nous ne savons pas ce que c'est qu'un discours sans *queue ni tête* aphalle et acéphale. Nous savons: c'est du non-sens. Mais nous ne savons pas: nous ne savons pas quoi faire du 'non-sens', nous n'y voyons pas plus loin que le bout de sens – Plato wants discourse to have the wellbuilt body of a large animal, with head, stomach and tail. So all of us, good Platonians of long standing, know and don't know what a discourse *lacking a head and tail* would be, acephalic and aphallic. We know it's non-sense, but we don't know what to make of this 'non-sense'; we don't see past the tip of sense." Jean-Luc Nancy, *Corpus*, trans. Richard A. Rand (New York: Fordham University Press, 2008), 12–13. (Italics in the original).

4 *Sprachfläche* – a term coined by Elfriede Jelinek to describe her work.

Schiller's language is certainly one barrier. It is just about the opposite of what we speak today – complex, intense and in rhyme. Its melodrama is alien and its syntax foreign: the unusually long, convoluted sentences, the alteration between prose and verse, the vocabulary, the choice of words. How can we speak such texts today? The very words shut us out. They do not want to leave our mouths. They pile up. For so long we have been accustomed to another kind of speaking, another kind of writing, another sentence structure, a different rhythm. Every era issues its own decrees. The media, not literature, now shape our use of language and set the paradigms. Texts are expected to be short and somehow cool, easygoing. Close to daily life. As distanced as possible, except for the teaser. Pointed, yes, ironic, yes, but still simple. By no means complex or complicated and certainly not melodramatic, whatever that might mean.

The second barrier that makes it so difficult for Hannah J. is our historical distance from the piece. There is a need to go back in time, already evident in the play's title, *The Maid of Orleans: A Romantic Tragedy*, and in the description of the main character, "sainted virgin."

Tragedy. Romantic. Sainted. Virgin. Warrior. God's warrior – all words we took leave of long ago, words that now make us apprehensive. We are no longer innocent enough for them. They sound too political. Automatically, the hairs in our well-attuned ears stand on end. Various warning bells start ringing. We feel more comfortable with Bertolt Brecht's *Saint Joan of the Stockyards* in this regard. In contrast to the political systems envisioned by German idealism, in Brecht's version the word "saint" is legitimized through its proximity to the word "stockyards," reflecting the tremors of modernity, and the name shift from Joan of Arc to Johanna Dark evokes familiar terrain. "In my beginning is my end. [...] O dark, dark dark. They all go into the dark," writes T.S. Eliot in "East Coker."[5] That is something the citizens of postmodernity know well.

So how should a young actor who is just starting out, born long after 1968, find a way to embrace the particular events in and surrounding Schiller's Joan of Arc? Is that not by definition too much for her? Is there any way someone today could truly understand this phenomenon – God sending to a simple country girl a message that turns out to be

---

5   T.S. Eliot, "East Coker," in *Collected Poems 1909–1962* (London: Faber, 1963), 196–204.

a weighty political obligation – understand it viscerally and practically, not just on a theoretical level? Can we today still truly empathize with a young woman whose budding love for a man makes her feel guilty for betraying her divine mission? Does this make sense today, in feminist times, after the death of God and the subject, in an era of discourse and deconstruction?

All of these issues are discussed at great length and worked on extensively during rehearsals, over and over again, but to no avail. Hannah J. makes no headway in rolling this stone of Sisyphus up the mountain of the script; she tortures herself and those present. Schiller's words in her mouth are cumbersome and clumsy. The language, like the feelings it evokes, remains stuck in sentimentality. It is unbearable, "the intolerable and dishonest 'seriousness' of public and official rhetoric."[6] It is theater as a museum, nothing to write home about. Nothing is made conclusive, nothing permeable, nothing porous. The emotions and words have no effect on the audience, no bearing on their situation. The words do not lead into the complex world of their meanings. Their sense is hermetically sealed, robbed of all dimensionality, even though every word can be understood acoustically. No door is opened to Joan of Arc's world. No girl is created to whom heaven was revealed in the words of the archangels and who, under the banner of God, liberated France from the English and aided the coronation of the French king – a girl who now, on coronation day, on the day of victory and celebration, tries desperately to understand why, ever since she caught the cataclysmic look of love in the eyes of a man, the solid ground of her divine mission has turned into an abyss. Deeply upset, Joan the shepherdess, "Almighty God's own warrior," as Schiller has his main character say about herself, believes she is guilty, sullied by this glance of love – until she revolts against it. That is pretty much what this scene is about.

Nothing seems to emerge from this stagnation, but neither is there any protest against Schiller – not against his dramatic concept of the theater, which she could reject as anachronistic, nor against his language, which she could try to subvert, nor against his old-fashioned, reactionary image of women, which she could counter with noncompliance. Those would

---

6   Hans-Thies Lehmann, *Postdramatic Theatre*, trans. Karen Jurs-Mumby (New York: Routledge, 2006), 119.

be alternatives – a boycott by means of an aesthetic exploration, or by means of sociopolitical critique, since it is, in a way, an authoritative text with a humanistic educational ideal devoted to longing for the one and for the whole. But there is no trace of any of this. Instead, all we see is a drama student on stage, trying very hard. She has been trying hard for many rehearsals now. It is not pleasant to see this reflected in her face. The "no talent" verdict hangs in the air, that diffuse ghost that haunts so many beginners. Today, she seems to have reached the bottom. Rehearsals might be ended any second now. Why torture ourselves any longer?

Turning point, peripeteia

Suddenly, without any warning or transition, the situation on stage changes.

The young actor's figure grows – it becomes large, larger – it grows beyond its own actual size, suspends all perspective and – although she cannot lose her real size, her biological measurements – suddenly she fills the space; she penetrates the stage, feels it, fills it – until her limits burst, explode.

Simultaneously, a spell is cast, a temporal undertow – as if time had suddenly condensed, where only a second ago it was dragging on so laboriously. Boredom has disappeared completely now, as has dry uniformity. There is no longer a chronometer ticking out the seconds that march continuously straight ahead to the beat. Insubordinately they break rank, come together, become dense, denser, are torn apart and explode, like the space itself. Finally freed from linear order, time runs backward and forward simultaneously, jumps erratically. Past and future are both equally alive. It is as if time had been given wings.

The classroom has become still. No chairs move, and there are no hectic movements, no furtive glances toward the clock, no rustling of stealthy searches for chewing gum, a piece of candy, or some other trifle. All of that is forgotten. Not even a cell phone rings by mistake. All is silent now, everything hushed.

Irresistibly, the actor has gotten under the skin of everyone present. She is tangible now, close enough to touch. Her acting grabs and focuses everyone's attention, but without relying on the authority of a mimetically created illusion. No imaginary fourth wall has been erected by surprise, making for a kind of voyeuristic peephole into someone's intimate sphere. Something else is going on here. A completely different form of perception is gaining ground, taking over the space. It kindles a concentration that abruptly pulls everyone and everything into its magnetic field – the exact same interstice into which the actor herself has accidentally fallen has all of a sudden caught the audience by surprise.

A zoom without a camera, performed by the naked eye? Or has *Alice in Wonderland* taken over the auditorium unawares? Yet no potion has been drunk, not by anyone. There is not a bottle in sight. Nothing labeled *Drink me!* in large clear letters, every sip of which carries inexplicable consequences.

Until just a second ago, the rehearsal was plodding, uninspired, and boring; it was unbearably obedient – a dead end. Everyone present was distracted, bored to distraction. Resignation was widespread. The actor on stage was and remained a nondescript, commonplace apparition with no charisma, not the least bit interesting. There was nothing to do about it. She obviously did not feel comfortable in her own body, and she projected this disagreeably to the audience. You literally lost sight of her, as if she were not there at all. The stage knows no pity. She looked lost and small, her face was cramped and disfigured from the exertion of playing a role, which forces emotions, creates them, holds them up, suppressing, undermining, manipulating, and interrupting her own impulses as enemies. All help offered came to nothing. Not knowing what else to do, everyone had been about to give up.

And now – abruptly – unexpectedly, with no warning – this transformation into the opposite.

All past misery is liquidated. The figure on stage no longer seems nondescript, her face no longer cramped, but clear, lively, diaphanous. All at once. Language and words open up. All strain is lifted. The words flow swiftly, playfully, as if they had just been formed. They reanimate the body from head to toe. Every emotion is visible, each thought effortless. There are no annoying grimaces, no forced theatricality. Nothing is obtrusive. An easy intimacy awakens all the senses. An intimacy permeates the room and makes what is happening complex and multifaceted, almost tangible. At the same time, this closeness obscures the events, so that beyond sight, beyond hearing, beyond taste and touch and smell, their meanings elude us, revealing themselves only in their absence, in their silence. The event of the play evokes and revokes, hides and reveals, becomes a curly question mark that the audience cannot escape. Reversing inside and outside, its borders blur like time, or like the very space of the moment, without dissolving their differences into the diffuse.

Is this Joan's "forbidden" glance of love, about which Schiller has her say, while wrestling with herself: "It was with your glance that your crime began"?[7]

Turn around

Right in the middle of this liberated expanding and gathering, in the middle of this dissolution of interior and exterior – in less than the blink of an eye – the next turn, the next wrinkle in time. This time it takes the form of a demolition, a completely unexpected interruption of play. Over. Finito. Done. Curtain! Abruptly, with no warning, unforeseeable. It happens just as starkly as before, with just as little transition.

Why does Hannah J. stop?
Why now, at this moment of all times!

Anger wells up. Anger and frustration. Why is she willfully destroying the moment, just when her acting is truly felicitous? It is beyond comprehension. Ridiculous. Before, one would have understood. There were plenty of times when she could have stopped, when perhaps she even should have stopped. Everyone would have been relieved. Everyone was hoping she would stop. But now? Now of all times, the second everything starts going well! Why?

---

7   Schiller, Act IV, 775.

For no apparent reason, the actor on stage bursts into tears. But they are not Joan's tears; rather, they belong to Hannah J. Clearly flustered, she cannot carry on, cannot continue.

Once again, the auditorium becomes still. It is a different kind of stillness, an awkward stillness due to an incomprehensible, obviously intimate act that would have been better without witnesses. It is a confusing act, unsettling and not at all sentimental. Embarrassment is in the air. Nobody really knows what to do. But no one laughs or makes one of their usual jokes. The tense stillness continues. After a while the tension is broken by a tear-stained, but clearly stubborn voice that obstinately declares, much to the surprise of all present: "If that's acting, I don't know if I want to become an actor!" First there is surprise, then irritation.

A bizarre reversal. A strange and unexpected turnaround. It turns our expectations topsy-turvy; it is incomprehensible, disconcerting. To go through all that agony, to resist becoming discouraged and giving up when the play is going so badly and then, of all times, to stop when the play begins to flow! To break the effortless stream of creativity that cannot be constructed or made, that needs to come of its own. And instead of being happy to have felt it, instead of riding the wave, the kairos of the moment, there is obvious resistance, resistance so strong that it leads to an interruption of play, so strong that it makes Hannah J. break into tears and speak out against her own desire to become an actor.

Incomprehensible, paradoxical. Why should *accomplishment* provoke aversion? It was not failure, but success that made Hannah J. cry so that she stopped, had to stop and wanted to stop. But why? Why just when it was working? Why when her acting was fortunate and no longer unfortunate? What was it that made her cry? What was it that came over her? What beset her, scared her, frightened her? What turned the pleasure of her accomplishment into discontent, her felicity into infelicity?

Discreetly, the class leaves the rehearsal, leaving the student and her teacher alone.

i, mine

enough finito i've had enough i don't want to do this anymore this wasn't part of the deal are we being drugged here or what a play is play bullshit i have absolutely no desire anymore it's not cool or sexy or fun first it was frustrating really hard work and now my stomach is turning and my heart is pounding i don't understand what happened suddenly i'm not me anymore it's like someone's got the remote and I'm talking in tongues what are these words i'm suddenly thinking man does that sound stupid like i'm trying to be anyway what's wrong with me i'm not myself anymore ok that scares me makes me frantic as if i were me which i am what is it it's like it's kind of like i'm as if i'd been turned inside out

Nonsense! Outside is outside and inside is inside and I'm me. This is my head, these are my hands, these are my legs, this is my body. I can see it, I can touch it, this is me, three-dimensional, height times breadth times width, 120 pounds, 5'5" tall. Nothing has changed that. Nothing. Here I am, my name is Hannah J. Up to now I have always been able to rely on that. I can rely on that. My name is Hannah J. I've got my ID in my bag.

That's how it is.

Except where otherwise noted, this work is licensed under a Creative Commons Attribution 4.0 International License. To view a copy of this license, visit https://creativecommons.org/version4

OPEN

2
Speculations

Abstract: *The strange event, the acting student's paradoxical emotional reaction gives rise to a question. Why break out in tears of refusal in the very moment of creative, felicitous play? We are left thinking. What is the nature of the young actor's fear? What powers was she exposed to on stage? Did they trigger a memory from her childhood? What was going on inside her?*

Valerie, Susanne. *Actors and the Art of Performance: Under Exposure*. Basingstoke: Palgrave Macmillan, 2016. DOI: 10.1057/9781137596345.0007.

Actors' fears

What got into Hannah J.? This question hangs mockingly in the air long after the room is empty. Everyone is gone. Hannah J. and her teacher are gone too, after a long silence and a short conversation.

Uncharacteristically, someone has opened the window in the auditorium and turned off the lights. Usually everything is closed up tight, the air is unbearable, and all the lights are on. All the spotlights and all the ceiling lights are on, for no reason at all. But not this time. This time all the switches are off, and the window is wide open, as if the room needed fresh air, so as to more easily get a grip on leftover thoughts.

Ideas shoot back and forth to explain Hannah J.'s behavior. Thoughts cross each other, become superimposed, are released, let go of and picked up again. Despite misfiring, they press to be formulated; to be thought through and spelled out.

What drives an actor to stop playing in the middle of a scene? What makes her interrupt herself and perhaps even radically want to give up the profession?

The first spontaneous answer that comes to mind is failure. It is because her acting was no good, did not touch anyone, or because she was rejected. That sounds trivial. Everyone has trouble dealing with failure, not just actors. They do not have the sole rights on it. Of course not. But failure hits actors unfiltered. It touches their very self. There is nothing for them to hide behind. No medium comes between themselves and their acting, no tool, no instrument, no machine. They themselves are the "machines" that need to be turned on artistically. Their "material" is their own flesh and any problems that arise must be dealt with by the actor on stage, with "life and limb," *live* before the eyes and ears of others. For it is not theater or performance if others are not present to see. From the beginning, theater has needed spectators, eyewitnesses, an audience. But witnesses can praise or shame, can affirm or deny, can give a thumbs up or a thumbs down. Nobody is immune to this, nobody is spared, and there is no justice. None of this is new. Yet it continues to be underestimated.

Actors are subject to physical exposure. That may sound fairly harmless in theory, but it feels anything but harmless when you experience it on your own body. The intimacy on display is very fragile, and the risk is high and always volatile. There is no time lag, for everything takes place in the present moment. An actor can never discreetly hit "delete." He has always already been seen; he is always already under observation, whether in rehearsal or during performances. Only the actor can never see himself, not even back to front, as in a mirror. He can never take a step back to look at what he has done. He cannot give himself any distance. He is stuck with himself. He never sees his work with his own eyes. Only others see it. This makes actors, as it would make anyone, extremely dependent on whatever they hear about their own effect, and it makes them extremely sensitive.

There is hardly an actor who does not, if only silently, ask the muted question after the show: how did I do? It is a classic, a running gag among actors; everyone laughs about it. There is, of course, a comical side to it, something ludicrous, obsessive. But honestly, who can say that he is not susceptible to the echo of his performance, from the immediate applause to the later reviews? Who is not pleased? Who is not offended? Who is not affected? There are but a few who do not open the papers after a premiere, even if many deny it. There are but a few who have not turned to a new review with a gaze that takes on a life of its own, scanning the text for their own name.

It is easy to call this act of always first looking for one's self mere vanity and egoism. Vanity and egoism are common attributes among actors. Stereotypical ascriptions and expectations. Typical, you think, and are satisfied to think no further. What for? However, these stereotypes are not only unjust but also they hit the actor's sore spot. As Friedrich Nietzsche wrote about Richard Wagner, "You know not, who Wagner is: quite a great actor! [...] the greatest mime, the most astounding theatrical genius, [...] all he strains after is effect, nothing but effect."[1]

But to say Hannah J. is in love with herself, that she is a junkie for admiration, a junkie for success, does not help us understand what has happened. It does not help us grasp it. It does not get us anywhere. It makes no sense, even if we hear it in the media all the time. Because just a moment ago, Hannah J. was incredibly successful. The echo she

---

1 Friedrich Nietzsche, *The Case of Wagner, Nietzsche Contra Wagner, and Selected Aphorisms*, trans. Anthony Ludovici (Slough: Dodo Press, 2008), 11–12.

received from the concentrated silence of the audience signaled anything but failure.

Too bad. It would have been so easy to say a young drama student broke down in tears because her performance was completely amiss. That would have made logical sense. The actor stood up to the pressure for a long time, but now she has given in. She was crying because she was ashamed, because she felt like it was her fault. Ashamed ad personam, faulty ad personam. No matter how hard she tried, she played leadenly, again and again; she couldn't manage to meet the theatrical expectations. She just was not good enough, or not good enough yet. The role was too difficult or she was too bad – one or the other. There is no escaping negative self-scrutiny. The spectator at her back was all powerful. Her acting remained a wooden construct, forced. She knew it, but she could not change it and then she just wanted to give up; she couldn't go on anymore. Enough sweat and toil before all eyes with nothing to show for it. She ran out of energy. Tears welled up. She became more and more scared – scared of Joan's feelings, scared of Friedrich Schiller's language, scared of the text, of the next sentence, of the next word, of the next step. She became scared of the stage and scared of the theater; scared she would never get another role, or only small roles; scared that her dream of becoming an actor was maybe an illusion, that she had overestimated herself. She saved herself by crying – tears of failure; tears because she was a theatrical flop.

But the case of Hannah J. clearly broke this mold. Hannah J.'s reaction was divergent. Anachronistic. One and one do not make two. The logic is tangled. Its conclusion stutters. Had she not just overcome all her blocks, were not all her pores open, her acting inspired and suddenly skillful? Was her performance not beyond all expectations? There was no trace of failure. On the contrary. Hannah J. was exceptionally good. Yet still she broke down in tears and even felt compelled to give up her very desire to become an actor. It was as if she needed to defend herself from an attack.

Crying

Picture the French Revolution. It is the period after the September massacres. The revolutionaries have begun to target each other.

Maximilien de Robespierre has aided Georges Danton's demise. At dawn, Danton will die an ugly bloody death by the same guillotine that raged under his reign. Staring at the star-studded night sky, Georg Büchner (twenty-two years old, two years before his own untimely death) has Danton say, "The stars are scattered over the sky like shimmering tears; there must be deep sorrow in the eye from which they trickled."[2]

Suffering, worry, and sorrow turn beauty into horror. This elicits tears. Something rips, befalls you, shocks you, moves you, wounds you, exposes you. Something we have no control over. The pain is too great. Or the joy. Anger takes over, or impotence, rage, fear, desperation, grief. A hidden memory returns unbidden from oblivion or a realization shocks us and incites an inner war.

Tears can be bitter or sweet. Either way, tears tip the situation. Your eyes cloud over, you cannot see, and can barely talk. Tears signal a state of emergency, a cry for mercy, a means of asking others – and one's self – to show consideration. Tears are a way to lighten up and ease the pain. At the same time they are a barricade behind which you can hide, deflect the pain. The gaze is blurred, veiled by tears; they rob the eyes of sight. They make you blind. Emotionally blind? Blind to the reason for crying, even if it caused the tears? Do we cry for whatever cries out in pain, that which we do not want to acknowledge? There is an incongruity here, a paradox, a contradictory message. As the gaze clouds, a blind spot is revealed by the tears. Tears let us see what we have ignored; they show us the event affecting us in that moment.

> Deep down, deep down inside, the eye would be destined not to see but to weep. For at the very moment they veil sight, tears would unveil what is proper to the eye. And what they cause to surge up out of forgetfulness, there where the gaze or look looks after it, keeps it in reserve, would be nothing less than *aletheia*, the *truth* of the eyes [...].[3]

---

2 Georg Büchner, *Danton's Death*, trans. Henry J. Schmidt in Walter Hinderer and Henry J. Schmidt (eds.), *Georg Büchner. Complete Works and Letters* (New York: Continuum, 1986), Act IV, Scene III, 114.

3 Jacques Derrida, *Memoirs of the Blind,* trans. Pascale-Anne Brault and Michael Naas (Chicago: University of Chicago Press, 1993), 126. Italics in the original.

It is hard to ignore someone who is crying. They automatically grab our attention. Crying irritates us. Tears alarm us, even those of us who just happen to be there in whatever role, even that of gawker. Tears call out to the silent observer as much as to the adversary, involving both in the event they have triggered. Tears turn bystanders into participants, even when they turn away.

Crying disrupts daily life. It awakens dismay, pity, or disgust, even aversion. It makes us think, want to help. It makes us curious. Something is out of sync, derailed. *What happened?* The old question of *why* arises automatically. It will not leave us alone, demands to be assuaged. It wants to be solved, resolved, deciphered. Whether we want to or not, we relate the event to ourselves, try to make sense out of it for ourselves. We are driven by the need to find a key, a good ending, so that we can deal more appropriately with what has happened, or at least understand it better in retrospect. We tend to begin to speculate. We look around, peer in dark corners, run ideas by our inner eye *(speculari)*, weigh them, consider them, while always running the risk of missing things by a whisker, always ready to be determinedly wrong.

Speculations 21

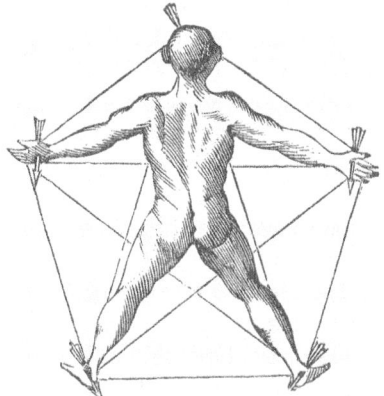

Figure 2.1 The image of the god Veivovis (Mars) was used by the ancient Egyptians as an image for bad luck.

Giordano Bruno, *De monade numero et figura liber* consequens de minimo magno et mensura, 1591: fol. 91. Courtesy of Heidelberg University Library, M 344-5-6 RES.

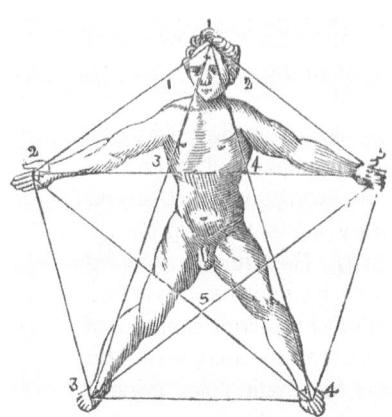

Figure 2.2 While the image of Diovis (Jupiter) stood for good luck.

Giordano Bruno, *De monade numero et figura liber* consequens de minimo magno et mensura: fol. 92. Courtesy of Heidelberg University Library, M 344-5-6 RES.

Child's play

The first letters. A, B, C. Thin lines, straight and curved, become letters in a fixed order. ABCDEFGHIJKLMNOPQRSTUVWXYZ. Twenty-six, no more. From these 2 x 13 letters words grow, first sentences. The fascination of reading and writing.

In made-up tirades a child plays what they have just learned. Spell house. H O U S E. Good, again. HOUSE. Very good, now I can doooo it!! Househousehousehousehouse. A tower of syllables. Househousehousehousehouse? Crazy word monster, it sounds so funny. househousehousehousehouse. House? What is a house? The meaning of the letters gets lost in their repetition. A house is a house is a house is a house! And a rose is a rose is a rose is a rose, says Gertrud Stein, the early messenger of enigmatic texts, spiral sentences that turn and turn until they come to a kind of linguistic standstill. "Play, play every day, play and play and play away, and then play the play you played to-day, the play you play every day, play it and play it."* Now I don't understand anything anymore.

Language, otherwise always at their disposal, has dissolved, its syntax shaken, they can no longer depend on the words, which become a convention, arbitrary signs that signify an agreed-upon meaning. Repeating a word shrinks its meaning until it dissolves. The letters seem strange, standing in a line, drained of meaning until they become meaningless. The madness of possibility, fascinating play, contradictory meaning are presented by a present of

---

* Gertrude Stein, *A Stein Reader*, Ulla E. Dydo (ed.) (Evanston, IL: Northwestern University Press, 1993), 147–148.

Exposed

The search engine cannot be turned off. It spins its web of thoughts – ruminations about the past, or protest about the present, or desire for the future, depending. The search machine continues in pursuit of Hannah J.'s tears and the taboo area that was touched upon.

Back to the beginning. Slowly. Step by step. What happened in auditorium X? What exactly did we observe?

Just when it had basically been decided that the play should be stopped, when everyone had secretly given up on any more attempts, there was a startling turn of events.

It was as if a railway switch had suddenly jumped over by itself, and unexpectedly the event of playing a role took hold of Hannah J., "kidnapped" her as it were (why not, kidnapped fits well), and all that had been a cramped struggle, the *effort* of her attempts, disappeared – and the play, thus freed, suddenly became ecstatic.

Failure turned into its opposite. One could also say the moment of resignation[4] was identical with the moment in which the will stopped trying to rule over the play, or vice versa, the moment of resignation coincided with the moment in which control over the play was taken away from the will.

And yet, unexpectedly, the kairos[5] of the play did not bring joy or happiness to the young actor but led her, on the contrary, to tears and defensiveness. Misfortune. It was as if the propitious moment of felicitous

---

4 Arno Böhler, *Politiken der Re-Signation: Derrida – Adorno* (Vienna: Turia & Kant, 2008).
5 Kairos, which stems from *keiro* (cut off) is related to *krinein* (separate, decide, judge). The substantive of *krinein* is *krisis*. *Krisis* is separation, a turning point. Kairos is time (*chronos*) cut in two halves, a before and an after. It is the middle (*metrion*) of time. Kairos as the crisis of *chronos* is a measure of time in the sense of *kriterion* and *metrion*. As a measure of time, kairos itself cannot be measured. For this reason, kairos not only had a practical meaning for the ancient Greeks but also an aesthetic meaning. As a measure it creates symmetry, beauty; it brings parts together, *harmonia*. It is a cut in the flow of *chronos*. In separating time it creates rhythm and thus harmonizes time that moves in different directions.

letters. Finding words, emptying words. Finding meaning, emptying meaning. Magic play in the playing field of being-in-the-world.

One of the first words a child learns to spell, a word that stands proudly in all school notebooks, is the word "I". The tiny word I in uncertain writing all down the line, an I and an asterisk alternate, along the first, the second, the third line down to the bottom margin of the page. I * I * I * I * I.

I, I, I, I I I I I I I I I I I I I I I I I I I. The child plays some more with the syllable tower, lets the letters gel, become an empty echo, topple, they are built up again with gusto, a hybrid form, I I I I I I, the letters become a monstrosity. Paralyzed, the child continues to play, I I I I I I I I I I I I I I I. I, the most affectionate of words. I, the word of identity, of unbroken unity, of self-conformity. *"I" that means me!*, the child suddenly realizes, *Imelmelmelme,* how strange it sounds, alien, threatening, and then it flashes, *I, who am I saying that to?* Instinctively, the child's hand moves to feel head. I, I'm saying that to myself.

Who is the addressee? Who is the addresser? These questions jump at the child from behind in the middle of playing, an ugly dwarf he suddenly has to carry.

Creation of the ego, dissolution of the ego. What has become inoperative? Who causes it? Me? Myself? Unsuspecting, in the middle of innocent play with harmless words, scary, strange, Ime. I'm becoming a stranger to myself, I'm becoming scared of myself. I me, Imelmelme.

Turned out of infant paradise, dropped and running – where to? Pulled where? Nowhere.

acting were not a gift offered to Hannah J., but, in an odd turnabout, constituted a kind of threat.

Assuming that Hannah J. did not overreact and become hysterical as a result of the release of the tension that had been building up so long, and assuming it was not just petulance, what was her misery made of? Was it the threat of being haunted by the specter of the art of acting? Was the sudden power of resignation in the middle of felicitous play overpowering, more difficult than failure in infelicitous play, because it broke an unspoken rule? Was it a taboo[6] that sought immediate revenge for having been broken by destabilizing Hannah J.'s idea of herself? Was it the fear that goes hand in hand with the "noblest of all nations, the resignation,"[7] as the philosophizing troublemaker Johann Nestroy ironically put it? Did fear begin to gnaw at the maxim of self-assuredness?

Does the acting ego, in the arms of passivity, no longer feel protected and grounded in free will, but instead feel as if it were random, contingent, and no longer positively identifiable? Where is it being led to? To nonsense?[8] Is it being led to where there is nothing to hold on to, where you are safe from nothing because the will is no longer dependable and logical reason no longer applies? Fear may have arisen unwittingly and unwillingly become part of a transformation machine, like for Alice in

---

6   "The meaning of "taboo," as we see it, diverges in two contrary directions. To us it means, on the one hand, "sacred," "consecrated," and on the other hand, "uncanny," "dangerous," "forbidden," "unclean." [...] Taboo prohibitions have no grounds and are of unknown origin. Though they are unintelligible to *us*, to those who are dominated by them they are taken as a matter of course." Sigmund Freud, *Totem and Taboo*, trans. James Strachey, *The Standard Edition of the Complete Psychological Works of Sigmund Freud*, vol. 13. (London: The Hogarth Press, 1971), 18.

7   "Comfort yourself with knowledge pussface and know: the most noble nation under the nations is the resignation." Johann Nestroy, *Das Mädl aus der Vorstadt* (Vienna: Anton Schroll & Co, 1962), Vol. 5, Act 1, Scene 12, 534.

8   "Hurry, hesitant Time, and bring them up against nonsense, / Else you'll warn them in vain what their good sense is about / Hurry, denature them wholly, up against frightful non-being / Bring them, or never they'll know just how denatured they are. / Never these fools will reform until they begin to feel giddy, / Never [recover their health] save in the stench of decay." "Prayer for the Incurable," in Friedrich Hölderlin, *Poems and Fragments*, trans. Michael Hamburger (London: Anvil Press Poetry, 2001), 59.

What wants me? The im-possibility of my existence? Completely beside myself, of my own doing, you should not eat the apple, the forbidden one. The Other in me, the phantom of my self. Am I my own undoing? What's come over me? The ego dissolved in an unending echo that takes meaning away from the familiar word. Close up. Silly game! All joy destroyed, every plus turned into a minus. Put through the wringer until there's nothing left, nothing, nothing at all. I disappear into nothing, black magic, correspondence with un-time.

An initial emergency of being. Whatever.

the rabbit hole.⁹ It may have been fear that embodying Schiller's Joan of Arc would be like jumping after a ridiculous white rabbit without wanting to,¹⁰ not literally, but in the action. Will you drive yourself crazy in the end? Will it be you standing at the final curtain? Or will you have been replaced by someone else?

it's like it's not me who's speaking, *i'm* no longer the subject, someone else is speaking through me¹¹ but it is me who's speaking, no one else but me, *i* speak *i* look *i* hear *i* smell *i* taste *i* feel *i'm* standing here on my own two feet *i* will now cross the stage

One's very self is threatened. The usual demands of the ego blow up a storm. *C'est moi, c'est moi!* you hear it call. But protest does not help. In the kairos of time the familiar order has run amok. A sore spot has been reached, an open boundary. The difference between interior and exterior you could always rely on has become tangled, all mixed up. You can no longer count on A being A or B being B, not that there is no counterpart, but the subject–object divide has disappeared, and other reference systems abound. Merde! Then the ego can do whatever it wants with itself. Create itself, destroy itself, be rid of itself. At any rate, it should take advantage of the situation because it has been offered a new career of unfettered freedom. No more constraints. No corset. No disciplinary action. No domestication. The belts and braces of all imaginary "upright holders"¹² have been cast aside. There is no one sitting in the control tower anymore. The windows and doors are open to the winds. The guy with the long white beard is long gone. And now his place is completely vacant. All authorities have disappeared, even the ego. The system has crashed. The game can only be played.

---

9   See, for example, Alice's musings in chapter 2 on whether she has perhaps turned into Ada or Mabel after falling down the rabbit hole. Lewis Carroll, *Alice's Adventures in Wonderland* (New York: Collier Books, 1962), 34.

10 Ibid., 22.

11 "The voice is a threshold phenomenon. ... Is the voice therefore the experience of the presence of an inaccessible Other?" Doris Kollesch and Sybille Krämer (eds.), *Stimme. Annäherung an eine Phänomen* (Frankfurt am Main: Suhrkamp, 2006), 12, 13.

12 See Klaas Huizing, *In Schrebers Garten* (Munich: Knaus Verlag, 2008). An "upright holder" (*Geradhalter*) is an apparatus invented by the German physician Daniel Gottlob Moritz Schreber to force children to sit upright at the table. His son, Daniel Paul Schreber, entered the history of psychoanalysis because his book *Memoirs of My Nervous Illness* was analyzed by Sigmund Freud in an early case history.

Did Musagete, god of poets and leader of the muses, change his lyre into a bow or his bow into a lyre in the kairos of the play? Is it time for a war or a wedding?

The poor ego gasps for air. It does not know what to do. Its imagination fails it. Struggling with itself, it is thrust into paralysis. Helpless, it collapses as its usual perceptions are turned around.

Both Joan's body, suddenly no longer caught between two book covers, and Schiller's language, no longer pressed between two lips, begin to rebel. They begin to act on their own, of their own will. They gain weight, put on pounds. They prop themselves up, are upheld, updated. No longer sanctioned by the ego, they subversively turn themselves over at the border crossing. They become spoken bodies, exscribed bodies.[13] Alien words for an alienating act. Our skin provides no more protection, no shield. There is nothing to hold on to, no dependable boundary. No limit to the self. No "Halt! This is where I begin. Come no further!" The skin is no longer the border of the physis, but the site where it stretches, is crossed, and dissolves.

To be thrown off balance by the play that has been set free, plummeting without a plummet, caught in a dizzy spell. To an unknown X. To the unfoundation of one's being.

To suddenly become a stranger to yourself in the midst of playing. Against the tenet of the autonomy of the will, not to be able to get a grip, to lose yourself from sight, pushed aside ignominiously, no longer center stage, catapulted to the outer reaches – and the fear at the back of your head that you might lose yourself there. Sacrifice your self. Suffer the self-destruction of your own will. Your ego no longer the last bastion of certainty, but powerless and vulnerable. An open wound that hurts. A lacuna. A tear in the web of the consciousness that has reigned until this moment.

---

13 "We must begin [with] the *exscription* of our body [...]" Nancy, *Corpus*, 11.

"Who's to say that the passion for the literal can be controlled? That gaping and scarring will not break through to the real at any given moment."[14]

Was it this imposition of felicitous acting that made the actor break into tears and stop, that provoked a stubborn "no" to her former desire to become an actor?

– – –

To find yourself *beside yourself*. Child's play, incidental. As if you'd always been there. Not artificially forced and without any hysterics. No exaltedness, no fake theatrical aftertaste. No crutches of specious talent. None of that deceptive, mostly self-serving, affectedness. Let out of the cave of habitual perception into the surplus of play. By chance. As if by accident. In one instant pushed to the margins, the seams. An unnamed in-between. Between the lines, between the cracks, between the borders. Traveling in an imaginary Charon's boat?[15] Jean-Luc Nancy says in *Corpus*,

The a-part-self as departure is what's exposed. "Exposition" doesn't mean that intimacy is extracted from its withdrawal, and carried outside, put on display. "Exposition," on the contrary, means that expression itself is an intimacy and a withdrawal. The *a-apart-self* is [...] this vertiginous withdrawal *of* the self *from* the self that is needed to open the infinity of that withdrawal *all the way up to* self. The body is this departure of self to self.[16]

---

14 Ronell, Avital, *The Test Drive* (Champaign: University of Illinois Press, 2005), 280.

15 Charon the ferryman brings the shadows of the dead over the river Styx (or Acheron) to Hades, home of the dead. The dead then go down to Hades as shadows and phantoms (*eidola kamonton*). The god of the underworld, whose name, "Hades," probably means "that which is not visible," was only reluctantly called by name by the Greeks, most probably for fear of thus getting the attention of the horrible ruler of the dead. See Edward Tripp, *Collins Dictionary of Classical Mythology* (London: Collins, 2002).

16 Nancy, *Corpus*, 33. Italics in the original.

With-out me

no not like this not with me this wasn't part of the deal not like this you got that without me what would happen otherwise where will i be enough finito i've had enough i don't want to anymore what's this about anyway i thought it was about schiller's joan and now

If this is what Hannah J. thought, she was right. This is about Schiller's Joan of Arc. But not her literary fiction, which can be closed back into volume II after reading and put back onto the bookshelf unharmed. On stage it is not about an intellectual debate over Schiller's Joan, but about her embodiment in flesh and blood. On stage, it is about acting, as it is so aptly called, an animate act of surrender.

It is an act that requires the physical presence of actors who must risk themselves. In auditorium X, in this specific case, the presence of the drama student Hannah J. Her entire physical existence must come into play, with all of her senses, with everything she has – her entire concrete physical body, her embodied mind.[17] She cannot use a stand-in; there is nothing between her and the role. She herself, Hannah J., has to embody the part to be played, hand her body over to the part.

i should hand myself over to joan of arc you've got to be kidding I'm not myself my self is joan of arc if it's me then i should give myself to myself that's absurd without me count me out I'm not interested

Understandable. There is a momentous *malheur* associated with handing oneself over on stage, with stage delivery. Maybe we can express it this way from a modern, enlightened, perspective. It is not enough that the actor has to give up her expectation of autonomy to others in the exposure her profession demands, the *malheur* increases twofold. If *homo sapiens* actually does become *homo ludens*,[18] she is not only at the mercy of others

---

17 Erika Fischer-Lichte speaks of "embodied mind," which is exemplified and highlighted in the performing arts, reminding us that "body and mind cannot be separated from each other. Each is always already implied in the other.... Man is embodied mind. No human can be reduced just to body or mind... The mind cannot exist without the body; it articulates itself through physicality." Erika Fischer-Lichte, *The Transformative Power of Performance. A New Aesthetics*, trans. Saskya Iris Jain (London: Routledge, 2008), 99.

18 Johan Huizinga, *Homo Ludens: A Study of the Play Element in Culture* (Boston: Beacon Press 1968).

but also, paradoxically, of herself – of herself as the elementary medium of this self, highly virulent in play. A contradiction opens up. A structure that is within her and over which she has no control. Within the actor as (active) subject, the self becomes a virulent (passive) subiectum.[19]

That could have caused Hannah J.'s distress. It is as if she had suddenly understood that, although the creative power of the will plays an important role in acting, the actor is completely at the mercy of her in-between, the uncanniness of her own being. A place she cannot access. When and why and whether it will become creative remains forever in darkness, despite all practical knowledge and ability, despite all the know-how that actors can and must accumulate. Perhaps Hannah J. only realized in the act of felicitous acting that the art of acting reaches far more deeply into her own existence than she had thought. Because theater, like all art, is inextricably linked to the baring of one's soul – a step that can by no means be skipped. It is a hard life being an artist, one might answer drily. But before all eyes, with one's own body? Each time anew? For life? Do I really want to do that to myself?

Yet perhaps Hannah J.'s refusal had nothing to do with the theater. Maybe it was something even more terrifying that showed its face. Perhaps the actor's dilemma only revealed the dilemma faced by all *Homo sapiens*: the impossibility of catching up with the dark side of existence. The anxiety caused by our inability to be sure of what we are or of that which we have up until now believed ourselves to be. A dilemma that we usually keep tightly under cover, deny completely, so as not to release its explosive power.

"The enlightened phantasm of the power and superiority of self-consciousness dissolves in fright. The sublime nature of art as an object of aesthetic experience reminds us of the illusory nature of identity and self-consciousness, of the fragility of the subject, and bursts open all claims to dominion," writes Dieter Mersch in *Ereignis und Aura. Untersuchungen zu einer Ästhetik des Performativen* (Event and aura – studies in the aesthetics of the performative).[20]

---

19 "Subiectum" is a translation of *hypokeimenon* (that which lies below), which Aristotle understood both in terms of a logical subject (Phys. I 2, 185 a 32) and as a substance, i.e., the carrier of properties (Met. VII 3, 1029 a 1).

20 Dieter Mersch, *Ereignis und Aura, Untersuchungen zu einer Ästhetik des Performativen* (Frankfurt am Main: Suhrkamp Verlag, 2002), 135–136.

All things considered, why voluntarily choose to make a career out of acting? A career in which your self will be the battlefield. Why become an actor and expose yourself and your body to the threat inherent in the tension between availability and unavailability, between action and passion? Always in the real uncertainty of a moment of openness, or of a constant shortage or surplus, with no deciding between the two. And what is more, all this in an era in which passivity has lost its place, in which there is no more room for it in society. In an era in which pathos has been ruined and stigmatized, both politically and religiously, an era whose cardinal virtue is reason and in which the mathematization of concepts has precedence.

Maybe similar ideas suddenly went through Hannah J.'s head – not those words, but the feelings – and she warded them off. This was not what she thought being an actor would be like. Where exactly had she ended up? She did not want to be there. She got in accidently in the middle of playing. "I beg your pardon," Alice in Wonderland exclaimed as she zoomed down the hole. "I wonder if I shall fall right through the earth! How funny it'll seem to come out among the people that walk with their heads downward!"[21] In Georg Büchner's Lenz this sounds a bit darker: "He felt no fatigue, except sometimes it annoyed him that he could not walk on his head."[22]

But who wants to be able to walk with their head downward, with the sky as an abyss because they have mastered this fatal art? Who wants to fall through the earth? The a-logical is a mischief maker. Science is the era's ideal, the figure, the algorithm. Not the body, not the word, and most definitely not some dubious in-between. There is no doubt about this, no matter how much talk there is of differences. Yes is yes, and no is no. Round is not square, hot is not cold, you cannot put a square peg in a round hole, and I am I.

But what happens with everything that I do not think or say when it nevertheless comes knocking, threateningly? For example, in the act of acting in the theater, this suspicious, corrupt with-out me, is an act in which I, the offender, am no longer sure I am the only offender, and still there is no other offender in sight.

---

21 Carroll, 23. Italics in the original.
22 Georg Büchner, *Lenz*, trans. Richard Sieburth (New York: Archipelago Books, 2004), 3.

"How queer everything is today! And yesterday things went on just as usual. I wonder if I've been changed [...]? But if I'm not the same, the next question is, who in the world am I? Ah, that's the great puzzle!"[23]

But take this literally? Channel the forgotten? Ridiculous. No. Without me. No, most definitely no. "'For it might end,'" as Alice thought "'in my going out altogether like a candle. I wonder what I shall be like then.' And she tried to remember what the flame of a candle is like after the candle has been blown out, for she could not remember ever having seen such a thing."[24]

How do we react when our automatic behavior, our patterns, our clichés, our schemata,[25] no longer hold true? When the enlightened established order of who we are in the world loses its legitimacy – not abstractly, but physically – through that death in transformation that Heiner Müller defines as the core of theater.[26] How do we react? Do we hang up the phone to disconnect the unwanted call, the unsolicited intimacy of the numinous. *Exit tragoedia.* Quick, run! Out of here. Enough, finito. Curtain! These are other times. Disgusting, how could I get so close to myself?!

This tangled relationship to truth. This tangled relationship to the truth of play on stage.

"Once [...] I was a real turtle,"[27] the mock turtle says with tears in his eyes when Alice asks about his history.

---

23 Carroll, 4.
24 Ibid., 28.
25 Judith Butler, *Bodies That Matter* (Abingdon: Routledge, 1993); Arno Böhler, *Singularitäten. Von der erotischen Durchdringung der Leere* (Vienna: Passagen Verlag, 2005).
26 Alexander Kluge and Heiner Müller, *Ich bin ein Landvermesser. Gespräche mit Heiner Müller* (Hamburg: BEBUG mbH/ Rotbuch Verlag, 1996), 176.
27 Carroll, 118.

Except where otherwise noted, this work is licensed under a Creative Commons Attribution 4.0 International License. To view a copy of this license, visit https://creativecommons.org/version4

OPEN

3
Black Out

Abstract: *This chapter concerns a child's fascination and fear at experiencing the theater for the first time, where the uncanny erupts and enthralls.*

Valerie, Susanne. *Actors and the Art of Performance: Under Exposure.* Basingstoke: Palgrave Macmillan, 2016. DOI: 10.1057/9781137596345.0008.

First time at the theater

Faust is being played on stage. Not Johann Wolfgang von Goethe's Faust, but the *Historia and Tale of Doctor Johannes Faustus, the Sorcerer*. Traditionally, dramatizations of the old folk tale are performed with hand puppets. But not this time. This time, it is being played by actors, by real flesh-and-blood people, on a small picture-frame stage.

It is an adaptation for children, and it is a full house. The show is nearly over. The church bell has already begun to toll midnight – the time has come, and soon the devil will get Dr. Faustus. Only a few more tolls of the bell – one, two –

The play is staged as a series of short chronological scenes telling the tale of Johannes Faustus: how he studied theology, then medicine and astrology; how he received his master's degree and his doctorate; and how his lust for life and his insatiable thirst for knowledge slowly and inexorably led him to become a conjuror and necromancer. The plot is as follows:

After Faustus – together with some slap-happy revelers – has squandered his entire inheritance, he enlists the help of dark powers to conjure the devil at a crossing in the woods at midnight so that he might "have whatsoever his heart would wish or desire."*

The magic works, and the devil actually appears. At his second appearance in Faustus's study, he agrees to serve Faustus and fulfill his worldly desires, under one

---

* Jason Colavito (ed.), *The Faust Book* (Albany: Jason Colavita, 2011), 63.

condition: the wise and honorable Herr Doctor must give him his body and soul after a term of twenty-four years. Faustus agrees. The pact is made and signed in blood.

The devil keeps his promise. The twenty-four years go by in no time for Faustus, surrounded by luxury and fantastical black magic. Now the time has come. The countdown has begun. Faustus's last hour is coming to an end. He cannot stop time. The clock is already striking midnight – one, two, three, four –

The staging is naive. No trace of the multimedia age. Nevertheless it exerts a pull, at least upon one young member of the audience.

Perhaps this child is a little too young for the performance. At any rate they have only vaguely understood the details of the story. But story or no story, it is completely clear that it is Faustus's fate to be enslaved to a demonic power for ever and ever. The child is vulnerable to the preternatural, the threat of calamity, vulnerable to that which comes over us when we are unprotected. The aura of the demonic repels and at the same time enthralls the young spectator, who is simultaneously scared and fascinated, pulled more and more into the History of the Damnable Life and Deserved Death of Doctor John Faustus, as if it were a David Lynch movie. The distance to the stage shrinks, the events become more and more real, the figures gain factual existence.

The devil's first appearance in the midnight wood caught this naive audience member completely by surprise. Until that moment, the child had been watching guilelessly. Now the child waits breathlessly – as if also there with Faustus – for the devil's next appearance in the study. The adversary will arrive. Mephistopheles will show himself a second time to seal the agreed-upon pact. But when? When will it happen? When will it ultimately happen? And how? Which guise will the devil take this time? Waiting is almost a form of torture.

Then, around noon, a shadow peeks from behind the wood stove – only a shadow, a harmless shadow, the kind all objects make when the sun shines upon them. But the sun does not shine inside the room. The sun is over the house, at its peak. The shadow grows, becomes larger and larger, overgrowing the furnishings and the walls. It presses on your chest, takes your breath away. It weighs a ton, even though there is nothing there. Nothing; just dark air – no weight, just a shadow, just black.

The child stares hypnotically at the stage. Why is the shadow coming from behind the stove, of all places! That is sneaky, that is mean! The incongruity of the wood stove that promises warmth and the monstrous darkness behind chills to the bone. The cozy wood stove is no longer a safe harbor. Its familiar comfort is an empty promise. A mean trick? A trap? When a shapeless hybrid monster with a human head suddenly jumps out of the shadow, the child's imagination is no longer able to distinguish between real and fictive events.

Blackout.

When the child's eyes open again, instead of the human-headed beast, a monk in a grey cloak is standing there. A holy man of the cloth. A guarantor of good, who should bestow confidence. But the fear remains. It lingers. Has it been provoked by the knowledge that evil resides within the cloak in a terrible turn-around of holiness? Is it the mockery of God's omnipotence implicit in this manifestation of the devil, who by taking on the appearance of a monk has made himself sovereign over a perversion of the good? Is that what has crept into his bones and has become subcutaneously disturbing?

The child's belief in good, in the images of good passed down from generation to generation, is still intact, determined as it is by reliable experience. The earth carries us, the sun shines, you wake up every morning healthy and happy. Most of all, at home there is an unconditional hug always waiting to take you up and offer shelter. But it is not the inversion, the portrayal of evil in the sanctimonious mask of good that touches the child's deepest fear. That fear lies elsewhere.

There is a figure. But no face. Why is the monk hiding his face? What is lurking there? What is veiled in the obscurity of the pointed hood? – a hideous visage, a demon – or instead of a visage – uncanny and gloomy – nothing – simply nothing – if you would grasp at nothing. And your own hand moves toward it with a will of its own – at nothingness that grips you – toward which you are pulled – resistance is futile – pulled –

It is the blank space that makes the child come unstuck, the lacuna that bossily awakens the uncanny,* being at the mercy of a faceless power that sees without being seen. "This spectral someone other looks at us, we feel ourselves being looked at by it." Jacques

---

* Sigmund Freud, "The Uncanny," in *The Standard Edition of the Complete Psychological Works of Sigmund Freud*, XVII. ed. and trans. James Strachey et al. (London: The Hogarth Press, 1955), 218–252. Freud looks at meanings of the word "uncanny" (*unheimlich*) and contrasts them with meanings for the word "canny" (*heimlich, heimelig*).

Derrida calls this power of the specter the "visor effect."*

The floodgates of the imagination open, releasing non-stop images. It is bodily torture. Almost unbearable.

Faustus's final day has come. After a last meal for himself and his friends, he says goodbye and locks himself in his study. It is almost midnight. There's no escape. No safe haven in the eternal feminine, no arms to surround and protect. In this tale, only eternal damnation is waiting for Faustus. That is the horror, the perverseness of the idea of hell.

The church bell has begun to toll – it is almost midnight – one, two, three – at the last toll, at exactly twelve, Faustus's soul will fall forever into hell – four, five, six – the chronology of the bell's chimes is unstoppable; nothing can save him – seven, eight, nine – a thunderstorm breaks out in his study – a thunderstorm in a study? – desperate cries for help – ten, eleven, twelve.

Blackout.

The child comes to, crouched in its seat, head down, arms wrapped around legs for protection, while the other children all around clap, scream and laugh.

---

* Jacques Derrida, *Specters of Marx*, trans. Peggy Kamuf (New York: Routledge, 1994), 6. Italics in the original.

Except where otherwise noted, this work is licensed under a Creative Commons Attribution 4.0 International License. To view a copy of this license, visit https://creativecommons.org/version4

OPEN

Part II
Experts in Being?

OPEN

4
The Actor: A Creature of Fable

Abstract: *In Part II, the anachronistic conclusion is drawn that actors' exposure on stage, while they are engaged in the creative act, automatically catapults them into an awareness of the pathos of human existence. Actors, creatures of fable in a manner of speaking, affirm this knowledge and give themselves over to it on stage. As a result, actors become accountable for their art. The question becomes more pointed: why would one want to be an actor?*

Valerie, Susanne. *Actors and the Art of Performance: Under Exposure*. Basingstoke: Palgrave Macmillan, 2016. DOI: 10.1057/9781137596345.0010.

Why do you want to be an actor?

Back to the very first page, to the overused but stimulating question: *Why do you want to be an actor?* Back to the stream of all possible and impossible reasons for this desire, this dream, this felicitous and infelicitous act. Realistic and unrealistic associations flowed free and forthright while the writer was sitting at the computer of course, not lying on the analyst's couch, even though Sigmund Freud's study at Berggasse nineteen is only a stone's throw from here. But why should we curb our thoughts? Who could make us censor ourselves? There is no need to camouflage the paths our reflections take. Nobody is giving out grades, at least not in enlightened zones, they say. So why constrain ourselves? Why shouldn't the arts, why shouldn't artists, slip outside their time? After all, actors know all about slips, whether a banal *lapsus linguae* or a more dire, fatal mistake, like the bloody slip Penthesilea commits against Achilles, for which she finds only the words

So it was a mistake, a kiss a bite
The two should rhyme for one who truly loves
With all her heart can easily mistake them [...]
By Artemis my tongue pronounced one word
For sheer unbridled haste to say another[1]

Slips (of the tongue) are so common in the actor's art – why rein in our imagination if we want to understand the autotelos of the actor? Why not continue as we started, raving about where the actor comes from and where he is going, asking all we can of this fabled creature of truth? Why not? Why not play with the truth? Why not say about the pathos of his knowledge, his *nous pathetikos*, that he "posses[es] his pathos knowingly, insofar as the pathos would be an apprehension of existence returning upon itself"?[2] Could it be a site of remembrance, a reminder of what we, qua our existence, might have become? Why not?

Does the reining discourse hold dominion over us? The old discourse? The new one? The newest?

---

1   Heinrich von Kleist, *Penthesilea,* trans. James Agee (New York: Harpers, 1998), 184.

2   Pierre Klossowski, "Nietzsche, Polytheism and Parody," in *Bulletin de la Société Américaine de Philosophie de Langue Français.* Vol. 14/2 (Fall, 2004), 82–119, 94.

(incredulously) What?
Every era issues its own decrees?
I beg to differ!
(with a slightly mocking expression) Excuse me?
Every era has its holy cows?
(laughs) Bullshit!

So, is the actor a fabled creature of truth? No, not an animal in a fable (even if Aesop's fox and his friends are not the worst of roles), but himself fabulous because of his profession. What do we associate with the word "fable," without losing sight of the actor? The spontaneous answers: Stories, make-believe, tall tales, fake histories, fabrication, narration. All fits. But we also said "fabulous." Spectacular, legendary, fantastical, strike a pose. All good fits. And then there is fabulation. Fits. And the less well-known intransitive verb, to fable, derived of course from the stories themselves, to tell as if true, to lie. Also fits. And speaking of derivation, etymologically "fable, *fabula*, comes from the Latin verb *fari*, which means both 'to predict' and 'to rave' (prédire et divaguer); *fatum*, fate, is also the past participle of *fari*."[3] Now we are going out on a limb. When, pray tell, does an actor predict fate? Oedipus's guilt perhaps or Lear's madness? Or the end of bourgeois theater? Or of a consumer culture that has become completely blasé? Or...?

The zenith of our associations with the word fable is Friedrich Nietzsche's oft-cited aphorism "How the 'True World' Finally Became a Fable."[4] In this "History of an Error," the world, in an analogy with the history of creation, disappears in six historical phases. Successively, the perceptible world of phenomena and the imperceptible world of ideas slowly merge. At the end, at high noon, the two worlds, the true world and the apparent world, collapse and disappear into one another. The world is *refabulated*. It has again become a narrated event. The world's wheels of fortune or misfortune, of fate in all its variants and variations, turn. The world is again fabulous.

---

3 Ibid., 88.
4 Friedrich Nietzsche, *The Twilight of the Idols,* trans. Duncan Large (Oxford: Oxford University Press, 1998), 20. Hollingdale, whose translation is otherwise used here, translates *Fabel* more freely as "myth."

"Thus when we say that the world has become fable, we are also saying that it is a *fatum*; one raves, but in raving one foretells and predicts fate."[5]

But if the world, as our merciful or unmerciful fate, appears only in the form of fables, only exists in the eventfulness of fabling, then who is that person whose art it is to tell – and live no less – about the world and our fate in it?

Assuming the actor is (perhaps) more than Nietzsche allows for in his *Daybreak: Thoughts on the Prejudices of Morality*, "They press close to the soul but not into the spirit of their object. [...] Let us never forget that the actor is no more than an ideal ape, and so much of an ape that he is incapable of believing in 'essence' or the 'essential': with him everything becomes play, word, gesture, stage, scenery and public."[6] If the actor can (perhaps) be more than this ideal ape, able to imitate so well, what *more* can he do?

Perhaps we need to look at this question together with the word "fable" and its meanings. Perhaps, Herr Professor Nietzsche, a somewhat brighter dawn?

In general, the actor is not a moralist. He is not interested in the *fabula docet*, the moral teachings of the beast fables of antiquity that have long belonged to the bourgeois canon. *Good* or *evil* are merely dramatic figures, not moral problems. But why not take a well-known beast fable as the beginning of an extramoral question?[7] What happens, for example, when we read Grimm's "The Hare and the Hedgehog" as a fable about the relationship of the actor to truth, lies and fiction?

What happens then?

The hare and the hedgehog make a bet about who can run faster. The wager makes no sense because the result is clear. But the cunning hedgehog starts the race knowing it is not necessarily a lost cause, because he has already positioned his wife at the finish line to wait for Mr. Longlegs. The hare, of course, cannot tell the difference between the two hedgehogs. The hedgehog wife is indistinguishable from her husband, and the

---

5   Klossowski, 88.

6   Friedrich Nietzsche, "Psychology of Actors," in *Daybreak: Thoughts on the Prejudices of Morality*, ed. Maudemarie Clark and Brian Leiter (Cambridge: Cambridge University Press, 1997), 160.

7   Friedrich Nietzsche. "On Truth and Lie in an Extra-Moral Sense," in *The Portable Nietzsche*, trans. Walter Kaufmann (New York: Viking Penguin, 1968), 42–47.

hedgehog wins despite his shorter legs. The hare cannot believe it and demands they start again. Dashing back and forth, he finally collapses from this identity runaround, because he can never distinguish the "true" hedgehog from the "false" hedgehog.

Read for the theater, this fable raises the question of whether actors also experience such an "identity runaround." Do actors also rush back and forth without any chance of winning until they drop dead of exhaustion?

Is the actor not in a similar fix as the arrogant hare, with the difference being that he himself is at both ends of the course? He is at once both hare and hedgehog, in constant competition with himself. He is, so to speak, his own opponent. He beats himself by fooling himself – because *he himself* is the site, medium, and intermediary of his play. Because *he himself,* his whole being from head to toe – his eyes, his nose, his mouth, his ears – depends upon, falls back upon, his own complex existence. But he can never catch sight of himself while he is playing, neither literally nor metaphorically.

This must cause a slew of questions to explode in the actor, be they ever so vague. What actually happens to the ego when an actor acts? What about the others? What about the character and his relationship to him, and to the characters of the other actors, as character and as himself? But even more disconcerting, almost alienating, what about his own ego in general? "Oh, to be someone else for once! Just for one minute," yearns Georg Büchner's Leonce.[8] Then he would be OK. But does not another contrary desire join this one that expresses itself thus: "Je est un autre."[9] Is the actor not haunted by multiple persons who speak through him and monkey about in the shadows? Among these persons are many whose visors are down. Is the actor then many? Considering all this, who would not fall flat on his face, fall over backwards, fall headlong into disaster like the poor hare? Who is not lost in a labyrinth, in a runaround, because the concepts of the enlightened consciousness, of critical reflection and logical analysis, suddenly no longer help us to take control of the situation?

---

8 Georg Büchner, *Leonce and Lena,* trans. Henry J. Schmidt, in Hinderer and Schmidt (eds.), *Georg Büchner. Complete Works and Letters,* Act I Scene I, 166.

9 Arthur Rimbaud, "Lettre du voyant" (letter to Paul Demeny), May 15, 1871, in Walter Jens (ed.), *Neues Literatur-Lexikon.* Vol. 14 (Munich: Kindler Verlag, 1996), 156.

Never mind the fact that we have cast our vote for emancipation.

In playing, the actor is in the grip of the dark, repressed knowledge of pathos. And pathos does not have much of a reputation anymore. Nevertheless it permeates the actor. Literally. It attacks him. Intractable, it awakens "that which cannot be explained by Reason or Understanding," as Johann Wolfgang von Goethe said of the demonic in his *Conversations with Johann Peter Eckerman*.[10] And he stresses that he does *not* mean Mephistopheles, who is too negative. Nothing could be further from his mind than the nihilism of Mephistopheles, who believes that everything that has been created should be destroyed. Rather the demonic is, according to Goethe, an active, affirmative power, a creative power.

Now let us go back to the question of why people might want to become actors.

Could it not have something to do with this demonic power, this dubious, emotional zone beyond reason, unreasonable? Does this demonic power exert a seductive, erotic pull that makes people want to become actors? It is the liberation from the law of identity. *A* does not have to be *A*, but can also be *A* plus *n*. Is that not the underlying desire for and fascination with the stage? And, at the same time, is not the demonic – the erotic act of play that couples the canny with the uncanny[11] – also the distinctive eros of the actor? Is that not the nature of the eros that, in the end, draws in the audience? Eros, the Greek daimon of love; Eros as a medium, the middle, the intermediary, the mediator between knowing and unknowing, between phenomena and ideas, "spans the chasm that divides them and therefore in him all is bound together."[12] This is the source of the power and the aura of all theater. This is the event the audience perceives.

Perhaps we can describe the actor as a fabled creature of truth as follows: The actor as a creature of fable – remembering the common root of *fabula* and *fatum* – tells us the human fate of exposure to the world. But he tells us not only through the narrative – though he tells a story

---

10 Goethe, J.W. and Eckermann, J.P. *Conversations*, trans. John Oxenford (Cambridge: Da Capo Press, 1998), 392.
11 See again Freud's analysis of the etymology of the word "uncanny" in *The Uncanny*.
12 Plato, *Symposium*, trans. Benjamin Jowett (New York: Dover, 1993), 26.

whose fateful threads become visible to the audience as they are played. No, it is the actor himself in the act of acting whose body becomes the demonstrative site of the vulnerability of exposition. He is its mask, its face, its name – as if to remind us, as if to remind us of the specter, the spectacle of our being, before the eyes and ears of others.

The actor's demonic power is perhaps the way in which he brings together the canny and the uncanny. Perhaps he is an erote, a messenger of the fatality of our existence. Through his act of aisthesis, in his possession of the knowledge of pathos – laughing, cursing, murdering, whoring, stammering, praying, loving, truth saying, soothsaying – he reminds us that we cannot escape this facticity nor manage without it. That we can only, by playing masterfully, re-sign ourselves to it.

Except where otherwise noted, this work is licensed under a Creative Commons Attribution 4.0 International License. To view a copy of this license, visit https://creativecommons.org/version4

OPEN

5
The Causa Corpora

Abstract: *Unlike the technological virtual world, the world of the stage is exposed, and the individual body of every actor is vulnerable. Actors are confronted with the idiosyncrasies of the body. Actors are at their mercy. At the same time, the intelligence and dignity of their anatomy is obvious.*

Valerie, Susanne. *Actors and the Art of Performance: Under Exposure*. Basingstoke: Palgrave Macmillan, 2016. DOI: 10.1057/9781137596345.0011.

The kiss of Olympia

The marriage of man and machine, of the living and the mechanical, is a theme that has pervaded the history of science and of the fine arts, literature, and theater from the very beginning. It both fascinates and repels us; it is invigorating and vitiating.

"Ah–Ah–Ah," sighs the beautiful Olympia and gazes at the student Nathaniel "immovably in his face" – to the delight of Nathaniel, who has just declared his love for her. How else could Olympia look but immovable? She is a puppet, a marionette, a machine, an artificial prosthesis. But blinded by love, Nathaniel does not see how fixed her gaze is. He does not notice that he is staring into dead eyes, that Olympia does not return his gaze, that he is staring into nothingness. On the contrary. In his distorted perception, the dead gaze of the beautiful machine becomes the phantasm of his love. Only she understands him completely: "O thou splendid heavenly lady! Thou ray from the promised land of love – thou deep soul in which all my being is reflected."[1] These words and more he whispers, spellbound, as his burning lips meet hers – which are as cold as ice! "He felt himself overcome by horror, the legend of the dead bride darted suddenly through his mind."[2] This is E.T.A. Hoffmann's tale "The Sandman," which Freud uses for his interpretation of the uncanny.[3]

Finally, a kiss. At long last! Fantasized for so long, desired so greatly and then – instead of a soft warm mouth – ice-cold lips, without feeling, inanimate, almost dead. The idea of such a kiss is immediately repulsive to us, and the more realistic it is, the more revulsion it awakens. You feel it viscerally. Automatically your mouth, nose, and lips pull back in disgust. You have to shake yourself to get rid of the abhorrent sensation.

Nathaniel ignores all of his body's alarm signals with fatal results. Without his noticing it, his kiss transforms from a promise of love into a promise of death. His blind gaze into Olympia's empty eyes is a

---

1 E.T.A. Hoffmann, "The Sandman" in Hoffmann, *Two Mysterious Tales*, trans. John Oxenford (New York: Mondial, 2008), 3–42.
2 Ibid., 33.
3 Freud, *The Uncanny*.

foreshadowing of his own death; a moment's gaze into a death mask,[4] a disregarded memento mori.

The deadly fate thus sealed is revealed at the end of the story. Nathaniel seems to have recovered from his shock on learning that Olympia's heavenly visage was the wax face of an eyeless automaton. He is happily reunited with Clara, his clear-headed bride-to-be. They climb the town hall steeple, which casts a long dark shadow over the marketplace. Nathaniel takes an unfortunate peek through a telescope he happens to have in his pocket and is again thrust into delirium.[5] Delusional, he mistakes Clara for the puppet Olympia and tries to throw her from the tower. Not until the very last second is she saved by her brother, while Nathaniel himself jumps from the spire.

And so Nathaniel the man is shattered, just as Olympia is torn apart in a furious fight between her creators.

With one difference.

One end is bloody, the other is not. In one a human being breathes his last breath, while in the other the mechanics of an automaton are broken.

Machine against man

In the natural sciences, in the arts, and in daily life, humans have long become disembodied via technology, media, and virtual reality. Whether positive or negative, questions arise. Polemical responses proliferate. Trade actors for avatars? Trade poor theater for big budget productions? Trade theater machines for empty space? Administrative bureaucracy has become anonymized, leading to Kafkaesque loops at every telephone call. *Please press 1 if you... if you... please press 2, if you, if you,*

---

[4] See Jean-Luc Nancy, "Masked Imagination," chapter 6 in *The Ground of the Image*, trans. Jeff Fort (New York: Fordham University Press, 2005), 80–100.

[5] "Nathaniel mechanically put his hand into his breast pocket – he found Coppola's telescope, and pointed it to one side. Clara was in the way of the glass. His pulse and veins leapt convulsively. Pale as death, he stared at Clara, soon streams of fire flashed and glared from his rolling eyes, he roared frightfully, like a hunted beast. Then he sprang high into the air and, punctuating his words with horrible laughter, he shrieked out in a piercing tone, 'Spin round, wooden doll! – spin round!' Then seizing Clara with immense force, he tried to hurl her down." E.T.A. Hoffmann, *The Sandman*, 28.

please press, please press, 3, 4, 5 ... please hold the line, the next ... beep, beep, beep. Transplantation, organ trafficking, genetic modification, cloning, patients perpetually attached to machines. In some hip clubs, "chipping" or "tagging" is in. You can have a microchip implanted (long a common practice for animals) that gives you VIP status and saves you the bother of carrying a credit card or cash.[6] Big Brother is smiling. What else? Artificial Intelligence, computer games, Second Life, blogging, Twitter, Facebook, cybersex. There is no world like the virtual world.

Is the artificial human the definitive aim of evolution? Dream, phantom, shadow, angel, *Übermensch*, demon, Golem, Frankenstein, robot, cyborg, hybrid, avatar? Has there been a turn, have the old stories of transformation, Ovid's *Metamorphoses*, become a trope in new myths? Perhaps a manifesto by Donna Haraway? Is, for example, Lara Croft, that icon of computer game avatars, a feminist variant of Olympia? Seductively beautiful, seductively perfect. A feminine ideal. How many Nathaniels have already lain blindly at her feet? Virtually, of course, not in real life. In real life they would lie shattered on the pavement in a pool of blood, painfully distorted, a dead lump of flesh, perhaps with a broken skull, their brains running out. Not a pretty sight. Not at all. Reality has not been faked. A real hit. A painful hit. A deadly hit. Ah – Ah – Ah! As it is, our modern Nathaniels are safe in the virtual world, with no risk of a meeting in real life and its uncontrollable consequences. They sit in a comfortable chair in front of a computer. Maybe their hands sweat a little, maybe somewhere in their bodies they feel arousal. Sure, why not? the screen is the telescope that imagines female beauty for them.[7] But

---

6 For example, in the Netherlands (Rotterdam), Spain (Barcelona: Baja Beach Club), Scotland (Edinburgh: Bar Soba) and the United States (Miami: Amika Nightclub). See Harald Neuber, "Das Konto im Oberarm." http://www.heise.de/tp/r4/artikel/17/17707/1.html. Accessed August 25, 2015.

7 "He took up a little, very neatly constructed pocket telescope, and looked through the window to try it. [...] Involuntarily he looked into Spalanzani's room; Olympia was sitting as usual before the little table, with her arms laid upon it, and her hands folded. For the first time he could see the wondrous beauty in the shape of her face; only her eyes seemed to him singularly still and dead. Nevertheless, as he looked more keenly through the glass, it seemed to him as if moist moonbeams were rising in Olympia's eyes. It was as if the power of seeing were being kindled for the first time; her glances flashed with constantly increasing life. As if spellbound, Nathaniel reclined against the window, meditating on the charming Olympia." Hoffmann, *The Sandman*, 28.

unlike Nathaniel, at the end they turn it off with a click of the mouse, the software shuts down, the screen fades, and the machine powers down. They do not fall to a painful death. They are still alive and kicking. There is no pool of blood under them, at most a wet stain from Coke or beer or something else...

The actor's trump card

The physical body of the actor is the central cipher of the theater – his singular bodily presence of flesh and blood, the exposed vulnerability of a being that has a name and only one life. Even if the human body can be replicated and faked by means of technological reproducibility and virtual simulation – up to and including its complete absence, where the actor appears only as a non-presence[8] – the singularity of the actor at hand remains the fascination of the theater. Intractable, theater – disregarding the cultural phenomenon of increasing disembodiment – continues to insist on the physical presence of the actor, and thus on the idiosyncrasy of the body and the vulnerability of the flesh. On stage, there is no hiding, no making a taboo of or faking the body, its vulnerable exposure. The body is open to scrutiny. Either way.

In acting, the actor risks no less than life and limb. There is no safety net. You may, of course, roll your eyes and think, excuse me, which actor risks his life? That only happens in other arenas. Bloody, cruel, truly lethal. That is true, of course. And nevertheless, in his own sphere, the actor's ante is his self, from head to toe. That is what is at stake when the wheel of fortune turns. Maybe he is not a tightrope walker who risks falling to his death if he makes one false step, but he is in more danger than it might seem at first sight. Even if it is only theatrical blood, even if the dead stand up and take their bows when the performance is over, it is still legitimate to describe this playing with the truth as a violent physical act, maybe even as an act that perforates the skin.

---

8   See, for example, Martin Arnold *High Noon Loop* and *Deanimated: The Invisible Ghost* or Heiner Goebbels's new musical *Stifters Dinge*.

Why?

Acting demands that the body remembers and reactivates its porosity, that it again becomes permeable, that it opens all senses. This is not possible without power and prowess. Actors need to take their heads out of the sand, ignore conventions, and leave any resentment behind. Their eyes and ears must be open so that they can be all ear and all eye. Their breath, their speech, and their movements must flow freely. To achieve all this and more is, surprisingly, much more difficult than it sounds in theoretical musings. It is a drawn-out, denuding process.

European history of the analysis of the subject has favored analytical thinking over ecstatic corporeality. This is demonstrated on every stage and at every public appearance. It is demonstrated by those who step onto the stage, by everyone who has learned to understand the language of the body and not only that of discourse. Actors are a case in point. The actor cannot ignore his body nor does he have it completely under control. At the mercy of his own instability and fragility, he experiences in his own body that he is neither one of Heinrich von Kleist's marionettes, which, floating, ignores the laws of gravity, nor is he Kleist's fencing bear, which parries every thrust. Rather, he is painfully conscious of his place at the side of Kleist's graceful youth who has become aware of his gift of grace. When, however, the youth tries to secure this gift and prove to himself and the others that he has it, he has the misfortune of losing it completely:

> He was unable to duplicate the same movement. [...] An invisible and inexplicable power like an iron net seemed to seize upon the spontaneity of his bearing.[9]

No matter which way we look at it, no matter what we do, the fact remains that the exposure of being on stage is a highly vulnerable situation for all actors. They are exposed to the fear of, perhaps one could even say to the pain of, illusory omnipotence. Heiner Müller even goes so far as to say, in a discussion with Alexander Kluge, that one of the most important characteristics of theater is that it subjects both actors and audience to death:

---

9 Heinrich von Kleist, "On the Marionette Theatre," trans. Thomas G. Neumiller, *The Drama Review, The "Puppet" Issue* 4/16 (1972), 22–26.

The essence of theater is transformation. Death. And everyone's afraid of this final transformation, you can count on that fear, you can build on it. It's the actor's fear and the audience's fear. What's singular to theater is not the presence of the living actor, or the living audience. It's the presence of someone who could potentially die.[10]

This is theater's trump card: that it can, to the point of mortality, create universal porosity. On stage, we see with our own eyes just how exposed we humans are, how vulnerable our bodies. The actor demonstrates this exposure with his own flesh and blood, and when his acting succeeds, he reminds us of our condition. Theater gives his body back the singularity and dignity that are his birthright. Presented to us in the abstract, masked by the media, this is so quickly and so easily ignored, so brutally disregarded. The actor's vulnerability, his mortality, no longer get under our skin. They no longer come close. They remain abstract, merely theoretical.

The most extreme forms of postdramatic theater confront us directly with bodily pain as a warning signal, a reminder of the bareness of our existence. In them, the deformed, tortured body is exposed to the point where performer and audience are no longer able to stand it. They push the body to the boundary of its lethal endangerment.[11] These are archaic acts, inspired by Dionysian bacchanals. Think what you will of them. Every quest, every act of conjuring, every provocation of the offensive eventfulness of art must follow its own path, if it wants to follow a path at all. And not every one of these paths requires an actor. He can be replaced by other artists who work in other art forms, or in other, less threatening types of theater that use laypeople, experts of reality who are situated in daily life rather than in the performative arts, or by theatrical concepts with other aesthetic or political priorities that do not involve the embodied "apprehension of existence returning upon itself."[12] That is not everyone's thing. Then be my guest, Mr.

---

10 Kluge and Müller, *Ich bin ein Landvermesser*, 95.

11 See, for example, Viennese Actionism or, among others, Marina Abramovic's *Lips of Thomas* or *Rhythm 0*, the Societas Raffaeolo Sanzio company or the American performance artist Chris Burden's *Five-Day-Locker-Piece*, *Shoot* or *Through Night Softly*. Discussed in Fischer-Lichte, 90ff.

12 Klossowski, 94.

Everyone, Ms. Everyone, go ahead and download your private lives onto the stage.

This text is an unequivocal examination of the *professional* actor. Of his pathos. Of his pain. Of his felicity, his infelicity. Of the vulnerability of his flesh. Of his Dionysian fragmentation. Of his particular art and special ability, as aptly evoked by Jean-Luc Nancy in *Corpus*:

Jean-Luc Nancy: Corpus

We often tend to think that the body is a substance, that something bodily is substantial. And opposed to this, or elsewhere, under another rubric, there would be something else – for example something like the subject – that would not be substantial. I'd like to show that the body, if there is a bodily something, is not substantial, but a subject.[13]

---

13 Nancy, *Corpus*, 123.

OPEN

6
The Gift of Acting

Abstract: *This section deals with certain preconceptions concerning thought, affect, and physicality. The jouissance of actors at play is examined: the knowledge and intelligence of their bodies, and their linguistic abilities in dialogue and communication with one another, as well as the art within their repetitions. All of these qualities and skills are accompanied by a physical feeling of not being the sovereign subject of one's own acting. The embodied dispositif of the Enlightenment proves to be an illusion when tested on one's own body, a chimera that gets in the way of acting.*

Valerie, Susanne. *Actors and the Art of Performance: Under Exposure*. Basingstoke: Palgrave Macmillan, 2016. DOI: 10.1057/9781137596345.0012.

Skipping

Actors often step out of line. They are not necessarily protesting against anything in particular. Politics is not usually their strong point. They just do not like being domesticated. It is hard to be creative if you let yourself be constrained by society's rules. Creativity is always also about breaking rank. Hardly any artistic work can be done without fractures and fissures, without the desire for – and need of – a surplus of independence and freedom.

But what is it that leads actors in particular to fall out of line, to resist the restrictions of conformity? Do they share some characteristic that explains their penchant for this particular brand of insubordination?

Looking more closely at the idiom "to step out of line," it is interesting that disturbing the given order is combined with the verb to step. Despite the military drums that measure these steps, the image to which this idiom gives rise is not necessarily confrontational. Instead we visualize a superfluous, unruly sidestep, a liberation from constraint – twisting away, not putting up fists. If we think of a line dance, what does this sole dancer who disobeys the rules do? Before our inner eye, we see them leave the rigid formation, deviate from the choreography, and start to skip. Just because. Because it is fun and because being good and following orders is so boring, so monotonous. If you like, you can imagine a guileless gaze to go with this small skip, or a satisfied smile that comes from the pleasure of the unseemly.

When we look at it like this, the destructiveness of disturbance is playfully transformed into musical dissonance.

Read in this way, actors' general propensity to resist norms and transgress set rules can be seen as a kind of side-stepping leap. It is a guileless carrying-on that is driven by fantasy, by the joy of creation. It is the way children sometimes skip exuberantly when they have not yet been "tamed" and still playfully express their lust for life. Even Plato mentioned this tendency of the young to skip unexpectedly for no discernable reason: "For men say that the young of all creatures cannot be quiet in their bodies or in their voices; they are always wanting to move and cry out; some leaping and skipping, and overflowing with sportiveness and delight at something, others uttering all sorts of cries."[1] Sensible adults do not usually act this way. It would be improper and embarrassing. Adults may not always be well-mannered and demure, but they do not act like fools. That is what is expected of them and, of course, they fulfill these expectations. They follow the same drummer or perhaps the whistle. They march in rank and file if told to and even let themselves be drilled, whatever the cost. Children are not as easy to train. Discipline gets in their way. It conflicts with their need to move, to play. If you do not make them walk calmly beside you, they immediately start to skip and dance, or to dally. Just for fun, out of pure joy, for pleasure. They are driven by teeming, overflowing energy that cannot be administered and that no one can make money out of. There is no understanding this logically. That small, unplanned, extra skip just emerges for no evident reason, with no particular aim. It justifies itself, just as art and friendship exist for their own sake.

Can't the actor, *homo ludens*, be characterized by just this playful overflow? At work and at home, in disposition and habitus. Isn't his permanent openness to escapades the precise source of his creativity, which society half admires and envies and half disdains?

Max Reinhardt's language is strange to us today. We tend to be put off by the way he speaks, because the words he chooses no longer speak to us. Nevertheless, it is impossible not to repeat here the famous line from his "Rede über den Schauspieler," his lecture about acting held in 1928 at Columbia University:

> I believe in the immortality of the theater, it is the most joyous hideaway for all those who have secretly stuck their childhood into their pockets and run off with it, to play on to the end of their days.[2]

What else is Reinhardt talking about in this declaration of love other than the actor's talent for that superfluous, childish skip, the jump for joy

---

[1] Plato, *The Laws, Book II*, trans. Benjamin Jowett (New York: Prometheus Books, 2000), 34. See also Johannes Bilstein, "Spiel-Glück und Glücks-Spiele," in *Maske und Kothurn, Dies ist kein Spiel* 4 (2008), 69.

[2] Max Reinhardt, "Rede über den Schauspieler," in Hugo Fetting (ed.) *Leben für das Theater. Briefe, Reden, Aufsätze, Interviews, Gespräche, Auszüge aus Regiebüchern* (Berlin: Argon Verlag, 1989), 436.

that shifts the world and life itself back into the realm of the unpredictable? Whether it is a comedy or a tragedy, this fragility of the prescribed is not limited to any particular content or development. It is part of all performative power which, in actuality, becomes the act, the manifestation, the event.

Usually, actors do not advocate any explicitly political cause. But are they not nevertheless per se "political" insofar as we might consider them to be the subversive disrupters of any behavior that acquiesces with the system? No matter what the performance is about, is not their propensity for a surprise turn, an unpredictable, gratuitous jump, is not their overflowing imagination and everything that continually seduces them to make up their language and inflection, their movements and their acts, is not this their own special form of resistance to all prescribed ways of thinking, to all norm-referenced behavior? In that superfluous skip, are not actors able to use the opportunity for free play that has been granted to them, to indulge in a little distancing dance (*Dis-tanz*) against the metalanguage of marketization and efficiency that has begun to increasingly pressure and rule over us all?

Prejudice

Prejudices simplify. They pack a punch and therefore live long. You think you have risen above them, that they have died, and then they unexpectedly peek out from behind the wings, or from the heads and hearts of the actors in which they have been slumbering. They are just waiting for their cue. In this case, it is the prejudice against thinking. This antipathy has built itself a nice little nest. As if thinking were the enemy of artistic, and thus also of performative, talent. As if imagination and creativity were not just disturbed and inhibited by the act of thinking, but poisoned and thwarted. As if sensuousness competed with the intellect and one needed to secede from, or even be sacrificed to, the other.

"Don't think, play!" (*Denk' net, spü!*) is an admonition sometimes heard in the theaters of Vienna. Speaking of prejudice, perhaps this distaste for thinking is a Viennese phenomenon. Maybe it is in the Viennese blood, the blood of this city that is so head over heels in love with the theater. Maybe. Who knows? But what other city still calls its stars *Lieblinge*?

I have even heard one of these *darlings*, bumped into by accident, call out "don't push me, I'm a *Liebling*." But anecdotes aside, where else do people fight so vehemently about theater, where else are actors honored so publicly as in Vienna? In life and in death. Honorary members of the Burgtheater Vienna have the privilege of – it is true! – being laid out after death at the top of the theater's grand staircase. A black carpet replaces the red for the occasion, and the entrance is draped with silver-tasseled black velvet curtains. The gravity of the curtains and the change from the theater's usual red and gold to the black and silver of death creates a powerful effect. People automatically pause, stop what they are doing to look. It is impossible to ignore this signal. The Grim Reaper makes his presence known and evokes strong images. After an official mourning ceremony on the staircase, with much aplomb in the presence of members of the government and, of course, the Burgtheater board, the pallbearers perform a ritual circling of the theater accompanied by a band, colleagues, fans, and passersby. It even used to be customary for the procession to circle the theater three times.

This is how Vienna shows its love for its departed actors. Eros and Thanatos are, of course, particularly intimate to Vienna, the city of Sigmund Freud, which leads us to another way of reading the actor's old prejudice against thinking. Could it be the return of the repressed, emotional remnants of Austro–Catholic Baroque resistance against Prusso–Protestant intellectualization and ideologization of the performative arts?

Curtain on the small jumps and skips. Curtain on the escapades.

The idea that thinking is the enemy of performative talent is not only questionable but also worth interrogating. Moving beyond the countless anecdotes about Viennese theater and a possible geographical/cultural heritage, the question remains as to what practical value theoretical and aesthetic reflection might hold for actors. *Let others worry about that. I just want to act.* Why shouldn't we just preserve the proven division of labor and leave theory – *theoria* – to the directors, dramatic advisers, theater studies majors, and, last but not least, the arts and theater pages. Why? Because with time it makes a difference whether or not an actor has also been interested in theory, in the power of discourses past and present. And it makes not just a theoretical difference but also a difference in corporeal experience. This knowledge informs his acting. Slowly, successively, it becomes inscribed in his body whether or not he has tried out or ignored different aesthetic forms, whether he has asked or refrained from asking ethical questions, and whether and how he has answered the question of art. The answer he has given will give his face an expression, will make his body matter or not,[3] and with time, in the course of an actor's life, it will bring out the difference between one actor and another. You only need to watch the stage closely. This is not a moral judgment. Luckily, it takes all kinds.

The question remains of the concept of thinking that is inimical to actors. What do actors, and by no means only actors, mean by *thinking* when this prejudice takes hold of their heads and hearts?

Theater and thinking have long had an ambivalent relationship involving a conflict, the roots of which go back to antiquity.

On the one hand, ancient philosophers considered the act of thinking, in analogy to theater, as the practice of contemplation (*theoria*), in which the person philosophizing could, in a state of amazement (*thaumázeo*) apprehend the actual truth (*óntos on theós*). On the other hand, Plato in particular believed theater was the adversary of thinking because, due to its intimacy with the realm of the emotions, it is closest to that part of being human which is furthest removed from the best in us – the noetic realm of reason.[4]

Is this philosophy's early, precritical, defensive reaction to theater as the barbarism of affect – and has theater avenged the critical abilities of thought with an accusation of the tyranny of reason? Is this the fly in the ointment? What about the excluded middle? The devil only knows where the excluded middle has got to.

This is not to gloss over, ignore, or belittle the differences between the characteristics of philosophers and actors. These differences are valuable. Not everybody can or should be able to do everything. Different professions require different proclivities that must be defended, whether contentiously or with longing. But what are these characteristics?

---

3 Butler, *Bodies That Matter*.
4 Arno Böhler, "TheatrReales Denken," in idem., and Susanne Granzer (ed.), *Ereignis Denken. TheatRealität–Performanz–Ereignis* (Vienna: Passagen Verlag, 2009), 11.

Which traits does the actor acquire due to his profession and which the philosopher? And where are their respective blind spots? What is underexposed and ignored, because the thinker and the player are deaf to them, whether out of conviction or just the pretense that this or that ability is contraindicative and would not be good for their own profession?

What is this assumption grounded upon, this preconceived opinion, this ominous pool of mutual distrust? What do we stand to lose? What is shut out, forgotten? And what set in stone?

Subject-based thinking versus stage experience

The theatrical subject is not an autonomous subject. This is the disquieting, irritating experience of being on stage.

On a non-discursive level, this quickly becomes clear in the praxis of acting. The actor acts within his material embodiment; he cannot disregard it or skip over it. It makes him unable to cheat himself. He has obviously been given over to his body, and whatever else he does, he has to let it play. It has a say whether he likes it or not. Because of this "medial" character of acting, instrumental reason soon has to forfeit its position of authority. While the possibility of success is certainly related to the actor's ability and talent, it remains at the mercy of the fragile and lucky felicitousness of the performance. All actors, not just stage actors, must capitulate to the providence of felicitous success.

That rubs us the wrong way. The enlightenment idea of the subject is the other way around. Subjectivity is rather "the power of success – [...] the ability to let effective acts succeed. The name of this ability or power to permit success is 'reason.'"[5] Enlightenment as subject-based thinking thus means being liberated into the autonomy of our free will, given the all-encompassing power of reason.

Reason should guarantee that we can allow reality to succeed, that we can bring it under our subjective control. This is what we have learned; it

---

5 Christoph Menke, "Subjektivität und Gelingen: Adorno – Derrida," in Eva L.-Waniek and Erik M. Vogt (eds.), *Derrida und Adorno – Zur Aktualität von Dekonstruktion und Frankfurter Schule* (Vienna: Turia + Kant, 2008), 190. Unpublished translation by Gerrit Jackson.

is deeply ingrained in us. And in all truth, who can resist the exonerating prospect of holding the key to success in their own two hands? Every failure thus becomes something we have done and consequently something we can repair if we only enhance and develop our ability. That takes away the uncertain and tragic elements of living that sometimes befall us as if from some external source. In light of the blows and breakdowns that no doubt everyone knows, you have to admit that a "reason machine" sounds pretty attractive, a lot more seductive than being exposed to the unassailable difference that connects ability and felicitous success. It is much better to optimistically rescind the difference between ability and success, between talent and felicity and identify each separately, ignoring the uncontrolled overflow inherent to their connection. An apologetics of numerals quietly begins to thrive.

On this occasion, we might be proud to present Herr Calculator in a Viennese farce perhaps entitled Skirmish on Wall Street or Lady Luck's Frame of Mind. He is wearing a crown on his head that has slipped down at an angle and he looks a bit disheveled despite his custom-made suit and expensive tie. But he smiles unperturbed – and the public greets its *Liebling* with roaring applause. Curtain.

The concept of enlightenment as the "(affirmative) theory of the subject's power, of the subject as power"[6] still – despite critical theory, poststructuralism, and deconstruction – infiltrates the idea we have of ourselves. Its modern form, subject-based thinking, "reduces whatever it may encounter as the substance of a sensation or a thought [...] to the subject of this sensation or this thought."[7] And this reduction is the base from which we automatically create the soups and sauces of ideas. This return to enlightenment subject-based thinking is archived thought; it has already taken place in the past. It is history that has entered our bodies. We can observe it in our own habitus and that of others. Our flesh and blood is the site of this archive, whether we know it or not and whether we like it or not. Subject-based thinking is so ingrained it seems "natural" to us. It is our historical homestead, our *calvary*. It lives in the syntax of our language, in the underlying structure of subject and predicate, which suggests that "I" always "do" something, that "I"

---

6   Ibid., 189.
7   Ibid.

am master over "my" actions. Our grammar constantly turns us into perpetrators.[8]

Thus we break with and ignore everything to do with passivity, with the pathic, with everything that can and does befall us without warning. The ego is seen not only as the precondition of being able to feel something but also and at the same time as the cause of and reason for those feelings. However, while the ego *is* the precondition for being able to feel something, feelings do not introduce themselves; rather, we are overcome by them. We are stricken by them. Disappointment hurts, fear lames us, hate distorts us, and we are thrown into chaos. Calamities befall us; happiness is not something we can calculate, not even the happiness of the high card, the greatest number.

Theater is incendiary. It can inflame the enlightenment concept of the subject and the pragmatism of analytical abstract thought, which seeks to calm itself with quantifiable criteria. The stage attacks the dominance of such rational, causal thought. The ego is exposed; its sovereignty is assaulted, shaken at its core because of this vulnerable exposition. This is meant as a literal occurrence, not as a figurative image. A painful event that causes discomfort. Offends. The tower of our modern self-assurance begins to crack. Not theoretically, but dramatically, involving all senses. Physically, because on stage the actor has to deliver, with his own body, the tenacious problem of modernity's collective interpretation of the self. He is forced into facing the experience that the ego is not the master of its own house, that whether or not he succeeds is not a matter of free will. He has no control over it, and no normative structure in the world can give it to him. No talent, no system, no method. Whether or not his acting is felicitous is out of his hands and thus uncertain. It is bestowed upon him.

---

8   "Language belongs in its origin to the age of the most rudimentary form of psychology: we find ourselves in the midst of a rude fetishism when we call to mind the basic presuppositions of the metaphysics of language – which is to say, of *reason*. It is *this* which sees everywhere deed and doer; this which believes in will as cause in general; this which believes in the 'ego', in the ego as being, in the ego as substance, and which *projects* its belief in the ego-substance on to all things [...]." Friedrich Nietzsche, *Twilight of the Idols*, trans. R. J. Hollingdale (London: Penguin 1990), 48. Italics in the original.

This is the unexpected earnestness that the actor faces, the thorn in his flesh. Neither success nor failure can help him over this hurdle, and it is something that plagues his whole career, not just its beginnings.[9] Make no mistake about that. No matter how long an actor practices his art, no matter how much ability he acquires over time, no matter how well he masters the craft, he will never lose his own shadow. Whether or not his acting is felicitous will always be up in the air. The eventfulness of playing in the theater necessarily leads the actor to oscillate between power and impotence,[10] between activity and passivity, between being perpetrator and victim. In-between. These contradictions are inadequately, paradoxically bound to one another. Promising and ominous.

Master and servant

"'I'm my own master' said the servant, and cut off his foot."[11] That is Bertolt Brecht's caustic ironic comment on the subject of master and slave. Not a bad theatrical description of the *physical* attacks, the wounds inflicted upon the actor "by himself." For the prevailing subject, the discovery of the unassailable difference between ability and success, between power and impotence, between acting and being acted upon becomes a "bloody" self-injury. The ego is subjected to "amputation" of and by its own body, which rebels. Is it perhaps even "beheaded," cut down?

There is a German theater saying: "The other actors play the king." No one can act the role of ruler believably if his or her colleagues do not play along. Even the best actor is powerless to change that. The ego on stage is in a similar predicament. No one is letting him play king. It is not working. The ego, the king, has been dethroned. He is a servant in his own house, but it is not because of how colleagues are acting, or because of a critic who wrote a bad review, or a booing audience. No, it

---

9   These problems should not be confused with whether or not an actor has "talent." That is not what this is about. In this study of actors, their talent is a given.
10 Sybille Krämer, "Was ist ein Medium? Über Boten, Engel, Viren, Geld und andere Medien," in GRENZ-film (ed.), *Philosophy On Stage* (Vienna: Passagen Verlag, 2007).
11 Bertolt Brecht, *The Caucasian Chalk Circle*, trans. Stefan Brecht, (Oxford: Heinemann, 1976).

is a narcissistic wound that the subject inflicts upon itself. Threatened by its own self, it can no longer be sure of itself. Without wanting to, it becomes lost, loses itself. That is the wound.

The continuous acid test that the actor must undergo is that his profession *physically* forces him not only to endure but also to be the carrier of the unwelcome incursion of passivity. He is at the mercy of the paradox of doing and leaving be, and he must, if he is to act well, embody the creative fusion of *actio* and *passio* within his being.

Despite everything that has been said about the stage, one could at this point just shrug one's shoulders and retort that in the 21st century, the problems posed by the early modern concept of the subject have long been overcome. We have understood them, caught up with them, and gone beyond them. Why insist upon the actor's *embodied effect*?

Why?

Since the actor is our guinea pig, to answer why, we should examine the practice of theater and look at one of the problems we often see in beginners. A role is attempted for the first time. Preliminary stage directions are developed. During the rehearsals to follow, this first draft takes on a life of its own. Many young actors automatically follow these initial directions as if they were remote controlled. They stand at the same cue, sit down at the same cue, lie down at the same cue, and so forth (and their speech follows this same pattern). It is as if the directions were an invisible safety rail that they must hold on to, which gives them unfounded confidence in their vulnerable state. They follow the directions "without thinking," as we say. Extraordinarily, the actors themselves are unaware of this. It happens without their registering it. What is more, when the play begins to take off, beginners often return to the old stage directions. In an emotional situation, they seem to reappear by themselves and superimpose themselves on newer solutions.

In light of this phenomenon, with regard to a grand narrative such as the Enlightenment, we must ask, what is the inscription of a few hours compared to the inscription of a few centuries?

The theorist is in a different position. He is spared the passion of the actor. His performances are first and foremost conceptual, not sensate. He reflects humankind's historical self-interpretation from a distance. While these ideas befall the actor's body and grab him by the collar, the theorist keeps them at bay with his intellect, so he may understand them abstractly.

When the theorist questions the concept of the physical body, he can keep it from getting to his own body. He objectifies it reflectively, looks at it from the outside. That he thus disregards his own materiality is a fact that is usually overlooked. And the theorist, protected by the distance of reflection, can also overlook this fact, since he only thinks formally about the physical nature of his own subjectivity. His task is to fulfill the scientific maxim of objectivity; otherwise, his work is given no credence.

This is not to say that the theorist has no passion. But the historical/cultural placement of the ego outside the body means that the theoretician's body is only theoretically, not practically, in the line of fire of his thought. His battlefield is the paper, the computer screen; it is not (his own) flesh that is under attack.[12] To deconstruct a reigning discourse in writing is not the same as to correct, transform, and supplement it *physically*, with one's own body. This demands great exertion, because one's own phenomenal body,[13] with all historically contingent inscriptions, also plays a role. It must break all resistance, overcome all automatic behavior. The body starts acting up when forced to leave its usual, daily territory.[14] It expresses its own desires, begins to live an unwanted life of its own, which (usually) is not even noticed by the person himself, or, if so, only as a diffuse feeling of physical indisposition, as a feeling of embarrassment.

---

12 On the 20th-century rediscovery of the "flesh" as a philosophical category, see Maurice Merleau-Ponty, *The Visible and the Invisible*, trans. Alphonso Lingis (Evanston, IL: Northwestern University Press, 1968).

13 On the term "phenomenal body," see Fischer-Lichte, chapter 4. In this chapter she discusses the problem of the traditional dichotomy of body and mind in Western thought: "Man is embodied mind. [...] The mind cannot exist without the body; it articulates itself through physicality" (99). She sees an astonishing parallel in the work of the great man of Polish theater Jerzy Grotowski: "The actor no longer lends his body to an exclusively mental process but makes the mind appear through the body, thus granting the body agency" (82), and in the late philosophy of Merleau-Ponty in *The Visible and the Invisible*: "The body is always already connected to the world through its 'flesh.' [...] In this sense, the body transcends each of its instrumental and semiotic functions through its fleshiness" (83).

14 For example, the body that best fits today's fitness and beauty ideal is of limited use to meet the demands of theater. It is too hard, too impervious, a block of muscle that blocks the breath from flowing. Releasing these tensions and blockages takes hard work and patience.

"I wish you wouldn't keep appearing and vanishing so suddenly: you make one quite giddy," says Alice to the Cheshire Cat "'All right,' said the Cat; and this time it vanished quite slowly, beginning with the end of the tail, and ending with the grin, which remained some time after the rest of it had gone. 'Well! I've often seen a cat without a grin,' thought Alice; 'but a grin without a cat! It's the most curious thing I ever saw in my life!'"[15]

Reworking the cultural and personally codified archive in one's own body and replacing the significant material traces of the body's ritual repetitiveness, its norms and registers, with new ones *at the material site of their occurrence* is difficult, more difficult than one would imagine. This kind of deconstruction and critical transformation of one's own body hurts. It cannot occur without passion. It carries pathos in itself.

The actor is exposed by this pathos of the flesh. He cannot ignore it, cannot disregard his own materiality. He must be creative in the conditions of his own embodiment. There is no way he cannot literally trip over himself and fall. The physical exposition of his art automatically confronts him with all the phenomena of human existence, with all its individual, cultural, and historical inscriptions. And he must carry and deliver all of his "flaws" and all his "insights" within his own body.

For this reason, the figure of the actor is a good *subject* of study in the laboratory of being. The rejected and neglected passive side of our existence passes before our eyes; the actor makes us see the two-edged gift of the event of his exposure, so that we, like Alice in Wonderland, must admit to the subject's fear of and resistance to the jump down the rabbit hole into a world in which there can be a "grin without a cat," and so that we, like Alice, must concede that we have no control over success or failure, that we cannot optimistically abolish their difference, cannot rely solely on our autonomy. We are exposed to, and at the mercy of an Other, a stranger who has no name. And one fine day, this exposure will be final.

---

15 Carroll, 84.

In the end, the most powerful theatrical moments are maybe even enactments of the "death of the subject." And perhaps this staging, the pinnacle of what theater can be, is exactly what Heiner Müller means by death in transformation, for him a core element of theater that unites audience and actors in their fear of this transformation – because it is, at least, a fear we can count on.

Friedrich Nietzsche: The Twilight of the Idols

One has to learn to *see*, one has to learn to *think*, one has to learn to *speak* and *write*: the end in all three is a noble culture. – Learning to *see* – habituating the eye to repose, to patience, to letting things come to it; learning to defer judgment, to investigate and comprehend the individual case in all its aspects. This is the *first* preliminary schooling in spirituality: not to react immediately to a stimulus [...].[16]

---

16 Friedrich Nietzsche, *Twilight of the Idols*, 76. Italics in the original.

Bodies on stage

On stage, the imagined world and the reflexive distance it offers do not exist. The stage demands that the actor give his all, not just his intellect. His entire phenomenal body is needed, from head to toe; no part may be missing – the whole of his anatomy is required, as well as the bodies of the other cast members and, of course, those of the audience.

Theater is an *ecstatic* art. It is the actor's profession to stick his neck out, to risk his palpable body in the act of performing in front of spectators/witnesses. There is no hiding place, no procrastinating, no rewind or fast forward, no technical means of correction after the fact. What happens now has happened – time bursts open – creates a gap – an empty space – through and throughout the actor – the event of acting ambushes the actor suddenly and ruthlessly – and the idea of man as a sovereign subject becomes an obstacle to playing, a conflict.

As soon as someone acts seriously, not just fooling around and flirting with the art of theater, they feel the full brunt of what it means to have dedicated themselves to acting as an event. The paradigm for this phenomenon is the premiere. Premieres create incredible tension, even for those who are good at hiding it. The body automatically sends out uncontrollable signals. The actor's stomach becomes queasy, his hands sweat, his mouth is dry, and he has to pace back and forth or leave quickly because his bladder is bursting, again. The signs may differ, but all actors are nervous, be they beginners or old hands. Everyone's heart beats faster before they go out on the open stage, knowing that they will soon be exposed to the eyes of the public. Anyone who says otherwise is lying. The actor's body is in a state of alarm. The heart beats faster, the breath quickens, and there is an outpouring of adrenaline like before a date you have been anticipating or dreading, one where you do not know what is going to happen, but you would not miss it for the world. The prospect of this moment of unassailability both exerts a pull and repels. Fear and desire shake hands.

The dilemma faced by the modern, enlightened actor stems from the subcutaneous malignant paradox described above. The act of acting is per se in contradiction to the modern idea of the self, while it simultaneously and automatically draws from this archived idea of the self. This forces the actor into a peculiar physical state of passion. He cannot shed the skin of modernity; he is not a reptile. But at the same time, the creative event of acting insists on the porosity of his skin; it must be torn open ecstatically, become permeable. In the limelight of the stage, with no cloak of invisibility at hand, "naked" – no script in hand, no rostrum to hide behind, without the shield of scientific neutrality and with the pressure of performative quality – the traditional master–slave relationship of corporeality and intellect is instantly reversed.[17] The play can no longer be delivered from the spirits it has called. The body has been turned on; it surges, begins to duplicate itself – and there is no wise sorcerer in sight. He has vanished from the story. The body can only throw its own weight around; the body itself matters and acts on its own authority.[18] Usually a slave, a lowly apprentice, the body now takes over the controls. It has no shame and it has low standards. For example, it may act like a lump of clay. No matter how nicely it is talked to, despite all the cajoling, it may remain clumsy and wooden. Suddenly, novice actors have not two, but four arms and legs. *What do I do with my hands?* Everything becomes a problem. *They're suddenly dangling so weirdly like they don't belong to me, alien.* Just standing there without immediately putting his hands into his pockets – a favorite gesture of male novice actors – just standing there without looking like he has been bolted to the ground and without bolting, going to stand somewhere else because he just cannot bear it and feels like he has to do something; just standing can become the most difficult of tasks. It may sound hackneyed, but to be on stage, exposed to the eyes of others, and to "believably" act some daily task naturally, not cramped, not stiff, without clichés – simply but focused – is a higher art than is commonly believed. Actors experience the paradoxical phenomenon that a dominant will, the usual instrument of autonomous action, is counterproductive to engaging acting. The will gets in the way, literally. It initiates a process of self-observation that censors breathing and imagination. It is the critic who gives grades, the superego that appraises, argues, judges, and passes out sentences. Blocks are preprogrammed, innocence lost. At the same time, the actor depends upon his will. He needs it. Without it he cannot

---

17 On the transvaluation of the ideal body–mind relationship in Nietzsche's philosophy, see Volker Gerhardt, "Die 'große Vernunft' des Leibes. Ein Versuch über Zarathustras vierte Rede," in idem (ed.), Friedrich Nietzsche, *Also sprach Zarathustra* (Berlin: Akademie-Verlag, 2000), 123–163.

18 On the weight of the body, see Judith Butler, *Bodies That Matter* and Jean-Luc Nancy, *Corpus*.

act, cannot perform a single action. Even if he is *only* walking, he needs to know *why* he is walking and *where to*, or his walk has no destination or reason because he *wants* to express that this act of walking has no destination and no reason. Without willful acts, without intention, no play can be performed, much less repeated. Even in a happening, a happening is what is supposed to happen and its elements are all the playthings of the actor's intention.

Innocence of becoming

Simultaneous dependency on the effectiveness of and on the absence of the will is a paradoxical problem no intellect can solve. It throws the actor into a state of contradiction. The greatest contradiction is the fact that his regulatory reason, his *ratio*, cannot control his will and must make space for capricious fabulation. Without the power of imagination, without creative inventiveness – which, diametrically opposed to conceptual reason, never has an inkling of its "results" – there can be no artistic work.

But it is easier to write or read about this late modern collapse than to put it *into action* oneself. This is the apex, the raw nerve, of the art of acting. The highest demands are made of the professional actor – impossible for a lay actor – by the paradox present in every production. Every evening, in opposition to the mythology of modernity, he must surrender to the innocence of becoming.[19] Again and again he must willfully step into the voltage field of opposed poles, the conflicting powers of this innocence of becoming. The ability to meet this challenge is the actor's know-how (*techne*). It is a long way to the intentionless intention[20] of acting on stage.

---

19 "What alone can *our* teaching be – That no one *gives* a human being his qualities: not God, not society, not his parents or ancestors, not *he himself*" (the nonsensical idea; last rejected here was propounded as 'intelligible freedom' by Kant, and perhaps also by Plato before him). Friedrich Nietzsche, *Twilight of the Idols*, 65. Italics in the original.

20 For Immanuel Kant, pleasure, which determines taste, is completely uninteresting, a purposeless purposiveness. See Immanuel Kant, *Critique of the Power of Judgment*, trans. Paul Guyer (ed.) and Eric Matthews (Cambridge: Cambridge University Press, 2001), 89f.

But if you are only watching from below, it is difficult to understand the problems that arise. When an actor fails, you ask yourself *what's their problem up there on stage, it can't be that difficult.* When he is triumphant, you feel vindicated, because it looks so easy, so playfully easy. *Learning all those lines by heart, that's difficult! But walking, standing, sitting down at the right moment?*

There is an image that is quite popular among theater people for the art of innocence: the way a stagehand strolls across the stage. Nothing else happens, nothing more exciting. He just walks – and all eyes are suddenly upon him. Not because he has disrupted the rehearsal and everyone automatically looks to see who is bothering them and waits impatiently until he is finally backstage again. No, it is that there is something simply riveting about the way he does it, the way he just walks. *I can do that too*, you might think. *Anyone can do that. Walking, simply walking. We've all been walking since we were toddlers.* But the innocence of the layperson, who does not even realize he is being watched, is easily lost when for whatever reason he is required to play. Very easily. You only need to ask the layperson to *repeat* his perfect, suggestive stroll in the same way. Already you have brought him down to reality, mixed with astonishment at the fact that it really is not as easy as it looks. Because just strolling across stage as if you were that stagehand and also making all eyes fall on you curiously, this *innocence of the artist* must be ranked higher. Many requirements must be met by the *experts in being* on stage.

"Being on stage," as a performative art, cannot be achieved by systematically replacing professional actors with laypeople. Theater as a physical event, when it works, is high art and nothing to do with the expert hermetics often attributed to the professional actor. Acting is an act of extreme vulnerability and fragility. It is not that laypeople cannot exhibit these qualities, but rather that the qualities of laypeople and artists are not interchangeable. They should not be played off against each other. Neither resentment nor trendiness should have the last word, but instead curiosity about the diversity of aesthetic forms.

The crux of the problem – as regards professional acting – resides in the personal, conscious participation in walking, standing, talking, and so on. There is no action without an actor. Walking, standing, talking, and so forth cannot be done without some-body who walks, who stands, who talks. The infinitive is indeterminate, all action is abstract and meaningless when no-body is doing it. Without players, there is no play; physical presence is the fundamental element of theater. The stage needs people who walk, talk, and stand. Again, it requires flesh-and-blood actors from head to toe – and this two-sided, unrelinquishable condition is the root of all problems in acting.

It is not a pleasant feeling when the weight of your body, your body's matter, matters so much, when your body is suddenly confronted with its own intractability. Were you not done with that after puberty? Not only do the demands of acting and the gaze of the Others make your body self-conscious, make it suddenly feel like a block of wood, but the body itself also begins to act out its own particular blockades, the weak points that everyone likes to hide from themselves. It is embarrassing how much the body reveals. It tells intimate secrets the actor would prefer to keep hidden. What is more, contrary to the actor's intentions, it reproduces all sorts of clichés, all sorts of conventional, normed behavior he did not know, or would have denied, he carried in himself. It is terrible to watch yourself literally embodying individual and historical conditioning that you thought you had overcome, were sure you were free of. It is terrible that is just *happens,* although you know better. The body's memory just automatically acts and reacts the way men and women just are, the way they simply act and react.[21] This is not to say that theater does not work with the idiosyncrasies of the individual actors, with their differences, their contradictions, and their resistance. Of course it draws on the quirks and characteristics of people and thus works with the pleasure and critique of stereotypes and clichés. But in *this* interpretation of the actor's art, they do not stem from the exposition of a private sphere that cannot be invaded, but from a manner of playing. The actor is not, as it were, "authentically" presenting his own "empirical data." Acting in the sense of *poiesis* is dedicated to the open future. It does not only document the reality it portrays, it does not only mirror – in pain and joy – the past and present that has marked the person in his or her lifetime.

---

21 On the construction of gender norms, see Judith Butler, *Gender Trouble* (New York: Routledge, 1990).

Language and speaking

One of the characters in Peter Handke's *Voyage to the Sonorous Land or The Art of Asking* is named Parzifal. Parzifal cannot stand being questioned. He reacts aggressively to each question. Otherwise he has no words; he is silent. Only once, listening to a story about death, does he slowly begin to stutter and speak. But while speaking he is overcome, as if he had known, by a new frenzy. He is overtaken by a compulsion to speak. Phrase after phrase leaves his mouth; he cannot stop the flow. Fragments of prayers, advertisements, headlines, lines from songs, his speaking transforms into a ceaseless wave of meaningless words. It is as if he had been cursed, caught in a modern Tatarus. When he finally stops, exhausted, the conversation apparently continues in his head, a torture that again makes him frantic. Not until much later, almost at the end of the journey, is Parzifal saved from the heap of meaningless letters. He can suddenly listen. Speech comes to him, alien and familiar. He slowly constructs new words, letter for letter, discovering them as if for the first time. "Wind, Sky, Dust, Water."[22] The spoken is created through speaking. Parzifal can call it up so that when he says its name, it is there. Wide-eyed he speaks word by word by word.

The same irritating phenomenon that can be observed in movement on stage is observed in language. All acts associated with language that come to us so easily in our daily lives – speaking, hearing, answering, and even being silent – lose their naturalness. They are called into question, create surprisingly complex problems.

Debutant actors are confronted with the problem that their speech does not obey them. Above and beyond the question of function – the workings of the breathing and speaking apparatuses that must first be trained – they find that they cannot *speak*, that they cannot *hear*, that they are not able to *think* the text that they have learned. They speak without being involved in what they are saying at the moment in which they speak it, and as a result they do not really understand what they are saying. Because they are concentrating so much on themselves and on their acting, they tend to not really *listen* to what their partner is saying. He or she becomes a mere prompter. All their attention is focused on it's

---

22 Peter Handke, *Voyage to the Sonorous Land or The Art of Asking*, trans. Gitta Honegger (New Haven: Yale University Press, 1996), 61–62.

my turn soon, my text is coming, now I need to speak. They are absorbed by their own action, by *how* to "do" it, *how* to "shape" the next sentence, the next word. *O no, that horrible word is coming, the worst sentence. How can I say it so it sounds right?* In this way, the actor manipulates, illustrates, and illuminates, but he doesn't listen, so he can't *answer*. No dialogue is born, no shared imagination; one person does not inspire the other. Listening and answering, the central acts of all creative collaboration, are neglected, passed over. They become missed opportunities.

One could say that in speaking, he forgets to listen to the text, to what he is *saying*, saying *to* another actor. The spoken text is actually nothing but an answer to what has been heard and answered within the text. For this reason, actors often fail because their approach to language is too instrumental. If they are too interested in forming the text and not primarily in understanding its meaning, the latter is lost to them and to the audience. It becomes intangible. Words become empty shells, decorative sentences that taste like cardboard and are unable to develop performative power. What is said begins to merge with overemotionalism, which may be interesting at first but soon becomes boring.

It is always the same. The sovereignty of the will, its dominance and concurrent wish to succeed hinders the act of acting. As regards his body and his speech, the actor cannot get around the hurdle of his profession: that his role is not only to act but also to be a medium. There is no way to solve this problem "reasonably." He owns neither his body nor his speech, even if both belong to him. Like his body, his speech does not let him use it as he will. It refuses to be manipulated. It does not obey him. If he tries to exploit his speech, to force it, to wring meaning out of it, it turns against him and refuses to surrender. It flees into arbitrariness, striking, but simple. The words sound as if they had been learned by rote; they become wooden, painted. They illustrate their meaning but remain empty, mere black-and-white print. Oratory. What is said becomes empty rhetoric and cliché, text that obfuscates meaning.

In Austria, the infamous repertoire of director Fritz Kortner is often repeated in rehearsals as a kind of shorthand for confronting these problems: "Don't say *disgust and loathing* like it's a Jewish company!" Or "Stop playing oak-birch!" Isn't Kortner's snappy commentary also an example of all speaking without thinking? And don't "weighty oaks" and "whispering birches" also contain all of theater's false tones?

Of course, technical ability is important to felicitous speech and to speaking on stage. That is beyond a doubt, even if skill is losing its reputation. Without *techne*, without technical skills, without training, there would be no professional theater. An untrained voice that does not know about breathing and rhythm, that comes from the wrong place and does not project, will hardly be able to use its full facilities and will soon give up the ghost. When vocal cords are strained and overexploited, it hurts – both speaker and listener, whether because, for example, the actor's voice is in his throat and cannot resonate in his body, or because of the unthinking, inflationary use of language.

Two things are necessary at the same time – surrender to and respect for language. The actor must both give language itself center stage and at the same time dedicate his entire palpable body to language. He cannot own it or treat it with disrespect. In both cases it pulls away, lapses, remains bland, flat, without vigor, without flesh, without eventfulness. Speech and speaking will not be subjugated or held liable. They are very sensitive to being treated carelessly. The magical depths of theatrical speech and speaking are only plumbed in the word that the speaker sends out beyond himself into the fathomless profundity of the silent and invisible web of meanings that accompany it. This is the web every good actor spins, even in what he does not say, even in the unsayable. Only careful listening allows such speech to speak through the actor, not the other way round. It is speech that speaks.[23] No philosophical knowledge is needed to understand this, only experience. It is speech that, going through the actor – back and forth between presence and absence – strikes a chord. In the kairos of this speech, behind what is said there is a glimpse of its possible meaning and at the same time the impossibility of comprehension. "Wind, Sky, Dust, Water."

Digesting speech

To learn a text so that it can be repeated by heart means to hold it inside your body. To do so, it must be read, its words must be picked out, collected.[24] They must be brought in, committed to memory, scanned so to

---

23 On this, see Martin Heidegger, *On the Way to Language* (New York: Harper & Row, 1971).

24 The first meaning in most etymological dictionaries for the Greek verb *legein*, the root of the word lecture, the action of reading, is to pick out, to select, to collect, to enumerate,

speak, so that they can be repeated automatically. The text must be saved internally, so that it can be re-collected at will from this inner archive. The German phrase for "to learn by heart" is *auswendig lernen*, literally to learn by turning outward. Such learning turns both inward and outward. It is a process with two mutually reinforcing aspects that belong together.

Not until this process of incorporation is complete has the text been completely understood, not just by the intellect, but by the entire body. Incorporation of a text is a complex learning process that functions similarly to the digestive system.[25] It takes time. It is often misconceived as a mechanical act of repetition, tedious learning by rote as so many people remember doing at school.

But it is more than that. An actor needs to almost *eat* his text, and to do so with enjoyment, like a gourmet delicacy. He must chew slowly and thoroughly, and the more his appetite increases, the richer the text becomes. The nuances of flavor are only brought out by slow and repeated chewing. If in contrast an actor simply swallows his text quickly, or if he inhales it mechanically as quickly as possible, its quality is lost. It is understood only superficially. *Undigested.* Not until all of a text's elements have been broken down has it been processed completely. Only then can it be drawn from by an actor while playing, without effort, automatically and reliably. A text that has not been incorporated completely can disappear. In the heat of emotions it is forgotten. The actor's memory is a clean slate and his feelings have erased it. The actor draws a blank, as it is called. And even if he remembers his lines, the text is still only "hot air." The audience sees an excited actor, but does not really understand why. That is boring, and the audience soon loses interest. But if a text has been incorporated, remembered with the physical body, then affect, logic, and logos are joined and can be released to play at any time. The text can be repeated at will as if reinvented, as if it had just been found, giving pleasure to all. And it can be repeated not just once but again and again and again – without ever becoming rote or mechanical. And the more poetic a text it is, the richer it becomes through repetition, since more can be found and understood in it and thus played with all the more.

---

and only its second meaning is to say, to speak, to tell, to declare, etc. The substantive is *logos*.

25 On mind or spirit as a question of nutrition and digestion, see Friedrich Nietzsche, *Ecce Homo,* trans. Duncan Large (Oxford: Oxford University Press, 2007), 21f.

Counterwords

When speech is released into a state of suspension between the audible and the inaudible, the heard and the unheard of, it releases additional energy – at least for a moment. In that moment, the force of a single cry is enough to turn deathly emptiness into hope, or hope into deathly emptiness. Lucille's scream in Georg Büchner's drama about the French Revolution is such an outcry.[26] Historically, it is the senseless rebellion of the human being who believes he can perhaps stop death at the last second after all. But no one hears him, neither man nor God, and everything continues as usual. The clocks tick, the bees buzz, time trickles away and takes life with it. Camille dies his bloody death on the scaffold, as do Danton and the others. No scream can prevent it. But there is a word that can turn it around. Paul Celan calls it the "counterword, it is the word that cuts the 'string,' the word that no longer bows down before 'the bystanders and old war-horses of history.'"[27] Lucille dares to speak this counterword. At the very end of the play, sitting on the steps to the guillotine, she cries out to one of the revolutionary guards, "Long live the King!" Are these the words of one who has been driven mad by her lover's murder? Celan reads it differently, as an act of liberation, a step with a direction.

The counterword the actor is able to speak, that does not bow to the bystanders and old warhorses of contemporary or ancient theater history, is *how* Lucille's cries cry out. *How*, the manner in which this scream is screamed, can be an act of liberation. In this scream, the actor risks the bareness of existence without calculating the effect, not showing off her virtuosity, not following a particular method. This does not mean she has no knowledge of effect, virtuosity ,and methods, but that is not all.

The *how* of such a scream can cut the strings on which the automaton, man the marionette, dangles and opens onto a world that is also there, namely, a world that has not yet completely finished with its past, but where the past can continue to be written and where the sanctity of all

---

26 Georg Büchner, *Danton's Death*, trans. Henry J. Schmidt, in Walter Hinderer and Henry J. Schmidt (eds.) *Georg Büchner. Complete Works and Letters* (New York: The Continuum Publishing Company, 1986), 123.

27 Paul Celan, *The Meridian: Final Version, Drafts, Materials*, trans. Pierre Joris, Bernhard Böschenstein and Heino Schmull (eds.) (Stanford: Stanford University Press, 2011), 193.

possible futures has always already been violated and at the same time overtaken. This is the muse's view, the turn, the *breathturn* and the beauty of performative art.

It [beauty] steps forward namelessly as a secret: Its mysteries outline the "bareness of form." [...] It is part of, participates in, the uniqueness of the moment. For this reason it allows, beyond language, solely an imperative of showing: "look!" or "hear!"[28]

In light of the aesthetics of contemporary theater, again almost dogmatic in a perverse reversal, we can translate Lucille's cry "Long live the King!" as "Long live beauty!" This is not meant to conjure up some preserved yesteryear, to continue along Celan's lines. We are not paying homage to some ancien régime, but rather to a yet-to-come *régime de l'avenir*.

"Long live beauty" is a call to beauty that appears suddenly, a moment of extreme vulnerability and porosity. Beauty as a breathturn, attentive to the big affirmation.

Why do you want to be an actor?
Perhaps that is why.

The Other, the others

Theater needs counterparts, a face vis-à-vis. It needs the Other, the others. There is no theater without the presence of others. You need actors and audience. Theater is a shared art, based on shared corporeal presence, and is thus an art of the moment under the gaze of the Other.

Gazed-upon moments are always also risky moments. You can never know beforehand how they will be answered or what will come of them. If you open yourself to the gaze, you must surrender to a stranger, to an Other. That can have fatal consequences and trigger events you never would have thought of and cannot imagine beforehand. A momentary glance can change everything that has gone before – like Joan of Arc's look into the eyes of Lionel in Friedrich Schiller's *Maid of Orleans* – and

---

28 Dieter Mersch, "Schönheit oder die 'Blöße' der Form," in *Ereignis und Aura* (Frankfurt am Main: Suhrkamp, 2002), 127.

inadvertently make you face the tragedy and riddle of non-identity into which it plunges you. It can also bring to light that which might otherwise have remained hidden and untouched in the dark, because it is confrontational, painful, and threatening.

The power of the gaze can cause calamities. It can objectify others, betray, curse, and cut. As the saying goes, a look can even kill. One involuntary gaze into the eyes of Medusa can turn you to stone, and fear of the evil eye is found in almost all cultures reaching back to the beginning of history.

Another momentary gaze is needed for interplay on stage. This is another desire altogether. Perhaps it has its roots in the "penetrating eyes" related to Dionysus,[29] which inspire and are the source of the bottomless reservoir of creativity. It is a gaze meant to challenge, not harm, others, not even by the distortions of idealizing. It is open to and unafraid of the future, and is therefore not a slave to the prejudices that dazzle and delude us and judge Others without seeing what they can do. Instead, it is fundamentally welcoming to the Other and wants to open all options for him, make all avenues possible. Such a gaze is fundamentally generous and passionate, willing to risk a love-gaze and trusting that it will be able to distinguish strange from stranger, so that it does not expose itself naively to the destructive Other. And if Medusa does stare back – something that has been known to happen even in the most beauteous temples of the muses – the gaze is averted in time or lets itself come to the test. For who, in the kairos of time, has exhibited more potency – Eros the matchmaker or the demon Negativity?

When the interplay goes well, Eros has a good chance. In the kairos of the moment, the gazes of *homo ludens* lock on stage in the shared eros of the creativity of the muses. And what kind of coupling would it be if one cut the other off in the name of his own pleasure and advantage? That would be a poor showing and not a felicitous act, even if one of the two, much acclaimed, believed himself to be the winner.

Victorious moments, gazed upon in theater and smiled upon by the muses, have another look to them. They are not self-centered nor do they know self-denial. Rather they are fed by the understanding that

---

29 Walter Otto, *Dionysus Myth and Cult*, trans. Walter Palmer (Bloomington: Indiana University Press, 1965), 90.

each experiences his own potency only in collaboration with others, that couplings bring forth life and that the quality of one is dependent upon the quality of the other. But dependency does not, as is often believed, revoke freedom. In creative interplay, dependency is a prerequisite for maximal freedom, for the freedom of play. Actors know, or at least intuit "that the true site of originality and strength is neither the other nor myself, but our relation itself."[30]

"It is the originality of the relation which must be conquered" so that the play can be a success, a felicitous event. That is why the space surrounding actors' relationships is neither the ego of one nor the ego of the other, but their cusp, in between the two. It is the hyphen of the open moment that both separates and joins, like the fond gaze that enables both actors to transcend themselves in play(ing) without losing their own individuality. From the paradox of with-out me, a web is spun between them (Greek: hyphe-web, hyphen-together), held by the finest of threads, and when it works, "when the relation is original, then the stereotype is shaken, transcended, evacuated, and jealousy, for instance, has no more room in this relation without a site, without topos."[31] Response and responsibility meet.

When all senses are penetrated in this way, and one's very existence merges with others, doesn't it bring ethics and aesthetics in the closest proximity? Isn't one precondition of the art of ensemble acting a regard for the exposed defenselessness of the other(s) and respect for the face of the other?[32]

Through this connection, the actors break through, throw off the pretenses and prejudices their past has conditioned them to carry. Regarding one another, they give each other space, create a shared space, one through the other, for the unexpected, the unforeseeable, leading one another. This happens not only during rehearsal, when putting the play together, but also in every staging of the performance. Performative quality always necessitates drawing from the past and anticipating the

---

30 Roland Barthes, *A Lover's Discourse: Fragments*, trans. Richard Howard (Toronto: Harper Collins, 2001), 35.

31 Ibid., 35–36.

32 Emmanuel Levinas, "Exteriority and the Face," section III in *Totality and Infinity*, trans. Alphonso Lingus (Dordrecht: Kluwer Academic Publishers, 1991), 187–253.

future; it requires reliable memory, and an open playing ground, whether in the jungle or in the garden.

In terms of temporality, you could say that the event of acting always unifies past, present, and future.[33] Their fixed sequence is jumbled up in the kairos of time, becomes open, and is rejoined in each moment. The actors never stop wandering backward and forward with one another in a strange land, a no man's land, into the unknown. This unknown exerts a pull on all players who, in the sensate desire for growth, bend toward it and incorporate it. In their shared joy and in their shared fear they spend themselves and find themselves in the pathos of laughing and crying about exposing themselves so, knowing they are exposed together.

Post scriptum. Luckily, often enough the dilemma of exposure dissolves in the blink of an eye, in the spoken words. Actors wink at each other, and the prompt box of their mind sends sentences such as "I will show myself highly fed and lowly taught"[34] – by which all weight is thrown off and scampers away.

Affect versus thought

We need to return to the idea that thinking is the enemy of performative talent and that affect is the enemy of philosophical or scientific integrity. Why? Because preconceptions are tenacious and hard to exterminate. Borrowing from Nietzsche we can say they are as "ineradicable as the flea-beetle" and "live longest."[35] Of course, they are always playing games. They like to sneak in wherever they can, excrete their poison, let off steam. The advantage of this is clear. You yourself are not guilty, you have an excuse, a scapegoat. Sigmund Freud and Nietzsche shake hands with one another. They pronounced the correct diagnosis. *Ressentiment* and transference are the ruling powers, and we can only ever be relatively free of them: "*The spirit of revenge*, my friends, has so far been the subject of man's best reflection; and where there was suffering, one always wanted

---

33 On the ecstatic unity of temporality and the ordinary (vulgar) concept of time, see section IV of Martin Heidegger, *Being and Time*, trans. John MacQuarrie and Edward Robinson (New York: Harper & Row, 1962).

34 William Shakespeare, *All's Well That Ends Well*, in *The Illustrated Stratford Shakespeare* (London: Chancellor Press, 1992), 264–289.

35 Nietzsche, "Thus Spoke Zarathustra," in *The Portable Nietzsche*, 129.

punishment too."³⁶ Vindictiveness is powerful and tenacious. It rips the potential out of life, and can poison it permanently.

But if we look more closely at *actors and feelings* and start with the common reproach that actors are guided by their emotions, do we not have to admit that the actor's typical weak spot is, in truth, affect? Aren't actors always a little bit *too* loud, a little bit *too* excited, a little bit *too* weak of will, *too* worried about the impression they make? Aren't they all *too* ready to ride the waves of their emotions? Aren't their feelings always jumping here and there, unfaithful and dangerously easy to seduce? Aren't there enough contemporary examples of this in political history? Aren't actors per se refugees of reason?

The actor has spirit, but little conscience of the spirit. Always he has faith in that with which he inspires the most faith – faith in himself. Tomorrow he has a new faith and the day after tomorrow a newer one. He has quick senses [...] and capricious moods.³⁷

Or do we need to turn what we have said about the actor's disposition on its head and concede that the actor's occupation forces him to ride the waves of emotion? What else could he do? You cannot swim or act on dry land. Acting is overflowing, chaotic, passionate, peripheral and proliferative. Is there more? Not even Brecht could have worked with actor cut-outs. Only a philistine can therefore demand the following of an actor:

> First, the *collegium logicum.*
> There will your mind be drilled and braced,
> As if in Spanish boots 'twere laced,
> And thus to graver paces brought,
> 'Twill plod along the path of thought.³⁸

Isn't Mephistopheles' mockery reminiscent of the way actors ridicule theory? Doesn't he go on to say, "gray are all theories, / And green alone

---

36 Ibid., 252.
37 Ibid., 164.
38 Johann Wolfgang von Goethe, *Faust I*, trans. Bayard Taylor (Renaissance Classics, 2012), 63–64. Italics in the original.

Life's golden tree"?[39] Sitting in a musty study or going out and grabbing life by the horns – it is not really a hard choice. This comparison is illuminating. Book learning evokes the famulus Wagner from Goethe's *Faust,* a bone-dry, boring, bourgeois representative of reason. Not a very popular role. Immediately you think of the color gray. Already you have taken sides, and this time it is not the emotions that lose, but thinking. Yet Mephistopheles's mockery goes deeper. In his counsel to the student he is not mocking thinking as thinking per se, but a particular kind of thinking. He is ridiculing a manner of thought that abstracts from the physical, from the world of the senses, even if advice such as the following: "To lead the women, learn the special feeling! / Their everlasting aches and groans, / In thousand tones, / Have all one source, one mode of healing"[40] might cause the mouths of some of this ilk to water and their pants to secretly bulge. But didn't Eve and her apple bring all this sin and misery upon humankind?

Today, we can replace the rationalist image of thinking with an intellectualist[41] image that believes it can rigorously distinguish between the content and performance of the act. Intellectualist thinking establishes a hierarchy between speech and speaking. It insists on the purity of a true or false content independent of the situation, the context, the tonality, and the gesture inherent to a sentence. They play no role in creating meaning. The grammatical or pragmatic rules of language determine what is "true" and what is "false."

The famulus Wagner can breathe a sigh of relief.

Performative intelligence is intuitively opposed to this kind of theoretical thinking. It rightly senses that it is counterproductive in performative art. It curbs, restrains, and constrains creativity, even punishes it. Acting is not a logical mathematical problem that must add up to the sum of its parts. Its result cannot be calculated. It is sensuous, contradictory, performative, and ecstatic. It thus always also includes an incalculable, unpredictable moment, an increase of being. The result of a performance is not logical, but ontological. It cannot be summed up with

---

39 Ibid., 69.
40 Ibid., 68.
41 On the intellectualist image of language, see Sybille Krämer, *Sprache, Sprechakt, Kommunikation. Sprachtheoretische Positionen des 20. Jahrhunderts* (Frankfurt am Main: Suhrkamp Verlag, 2001).

arguments. Its character is more of an erotic nature. Desirable, coupled. Every performance is a copulation, a copula,[42] an *amour fou*.

But from the vantage point of the *collegium logicum* it is of course a threat, an aberration both parasitical and arbitrary. It is an epicenter of uselessness, and actors are the potential do-no-gooders; they are a luxury that productive members of society allow themselves. The principle of non-contradiction is ignored, the excluded middle forgotten. A is not A, but rather A plus n. The outcome is always wrong; miscalculations abound. Gaps appear, empty spaces, unexpected differences. This space of difference, this desired, hidden space of the incalculable, is the site of the treasure of the actor's performative art.

Now somebody lifts a finger admonishingly.

Is it the old doomsayer from before?

People are vindictive. Why not allow ourselves a small pleasure? How would the honorable famulus Wagner feel if he were on the receiving end of a droll speech such as that delivered by Mephistopheles to the student? Shocked, he would no doubt flee instantly into his lonesome room and pull the covers up over his head...

But who knows?

The performative is always full of surprises.

Mephistopheles's clever play with the traveling student is full of surprising turns. It is a wonderful example of the art of performative speech, which is why it so confuses the poor boy. In the end he no longer knows what is up or down. The devil's learned words have turned him topsy-turvy. The most confusing thing is not even *what* Mephistopheles says, but *how* he says it. It is the way he uses words and concepts to underscore his arguments that the student finds absurd, objectionable, even indecent. And it is the way he stares, laughs at the wrong time, and reaches for the student. That sets off the student's internal alarm, but he does not know where the fire is. Mephistopheles's arguments and proofs take on one meaning and then another. They vacillate, oscillate, like a true chameleon. They attack with an adroit sticky tongue, and the student falls for it each time. But the most confusing thing is that despite all the back and forth, the words and sentences remain logical in and of themselves. And so consistent! But *their sound, their sound, and all the other trappings!*

---

42 F.W.J. Schelling, *Über das Wesen der menschlichen Freiheit* (Frankfurt am Main: Suhrkamp Verlag, 1975), 38.

In the end, it is "like a dream" to the student.[43]

Can't we ourselves take a new turn here and "dream," even assert that within the event of acting, thinking and emotionality are intertwined in a fruitful intimate dynamic? And that this event is not about liberation from affect, but the cleansing of affect to reveal its thoroughly noble quality, its ennoblement.

But how exactly is this expressed in emotions? By regarding, by training regard for, others and their alterity. This slowly drains ressentiment of its poison. Face to face there can be no more objectification and no judgment. A gaze into the face of the Other and the response made has to do with respons-ibility. By sensitizing and training the senses in this way, the stage becomes the site of an ethics of responsivity, a site of experiencing and re-membering (anamneses) the importance of alterity. Preemptively.[44]

Would this not in the end be "like a dream" for us?

Thinking and acting

Both thinking and acting reject conformity and civility. It is useless to try to play one against the other. Neither takes well to being normed. And if they do subject themselves to social mores, they stop being playful and thoughtful; they stop going beyond themselves; they long no longer; they turn our minds to prisoners. Our intellect is tied up and enslaved. The "Spanish boots" have us under their heel. Thinking and playing are right where they want them: conformist, obedient, and ready to draw the right conclusions, just as Mephistopheles mockingly advises.

But this is the wrong track for acting and for thinking. Their path is different. Don't both need to give themselves up to pleasure in the event of playing, the event of thinking? Don't both want to go to the limits of their possibilities? Don't both want to challenge their times? Don't both dare to transcend their times? Aren't both obsessed with the unanswerable question of why something is something rather than nothing? Aren't their questions about the meaning of being human, the sense and senselessness of our existence, almost libidinous? Questions that point

---

43 Goethe, *Faust I*, 69.
44 See Mersch, *Ereignis und Aura*, 9–21.

continuously toward absence; toward openness and emptiness; toward freedom.

All actors (no matter what their type) who care about more than just their own pleasure, who believe not only that they have a fantastic job (which they do) but also that they are dedicated to the pleasure of art, agree that they must dedicate themselves to this openness, this free space, this porosity.

Actors can be "soothplayers,"[45] because they create transparency. They are artists who can be "transparency personified"[46] in the limelight, so that at the end it is not they but "the audience who go home as actors – that is, confirmed in their own ways as players; that only in this transparency [actors] created could they realize that this is what they themselves embody."[47]

Emulating and mirroring the world is important and engaging. The historical gaze, the mimetic copy are very useful. The knowledge and ability we draw from them deliver elementary tools for both thinking and acting. But the *libido* of acting and thinking is hardly satisfied by looking into the mirror, by mirroring the splendor and ruin of our world. Doesn't the event of thinking and the event of acting – in which past, present and future come together felicitously – necessarily cause a fracture in every observation based on constative observation? It is a fracture of continuity – a promise of "another beginning" *within* the world, *within* art. Not that either the world to date or its art has ever fallen into that fissure, but the self-conceptions that ruled them have often done so.

When thinking and acting become an event, there is always a connection to the invisible, the inaudible, the not-thought. There is a trace of the above-named copula, the connection, the link – or perhaps the covenant, the yoke, but not the yoke of oppression. Thinking and acting have no interest in force, in taming, or in imprisoning. Neither do they want to placate, reassure, or gloss over. They want to be a thorn in the flesh, a thorn of attentiveness, penetrating the crust to make it permeable, to open eyes and ears and to rupture the skin. In the event of

---

45 Peter Handke, 13.
46 Ibid., 14.
47 Ibid.

acting, as in the event of thinking, the body becomes porous, the skin a dissoluble boundary; an opening onto the exterior world. This does not have the calming effect of illusion; it packs a punch, it spares no one. The others also become porous, electrified, their lives lit up, turned upside down. A peripeteia of the body–mind (physio-logical) condition by remembering the ecstasy of our existence.

In the fairy tale, Snow White is kissed awake in the kairos of time after a hundred-year sleep and many senseless deaths in the hedge of thorns.
 Yes, maybe like that.
 We are simply fools of the theater.

Repetition

Wouldn't it be much more useful to learn by heart the lessons life teaches us, repeating them again and again rather than falling in love with and running after some foolish, senseless ideal? Instead of hoping that you could "see the top of [your] head for once."[48] Would that help us? In the end we would only have wasted time uselessly and, like Büchner's hero Danton, be sad about our lives:

But time loses us. It's very boring, always putting on the shirt first and the pants over it and going to bed at night and crawling out again in the morning and always putting one foot before the other – there's no hope that it will ever be any different. It's very sad; and that millions have done it this way and millions will keep on doing it – and, above all, that we're made up of two halves which do the same thing so that everything happens twice – that's very sad.[49]

Nonsense! cry the loudspeakers of the happy market economy.

The power of repetition is fatal – for happiness and for unhappiness. It swings back and forth from compulsion and virtual potency, between compulsive repetition and future faculties, between stencils and

---

48 Georg Büchner, *Leonce and Lena,* trans. Henry J. Schmidt, in Walter Hinderer and Henry J. Schmidt (eds.), *Georg Büchner. Complete Works and Letters* (New York: The Continuum Publishing Company, 1986) 165.

49 Georg Büchner, *Danton's Death*, in *Georg Büchner. Complete Works and Letters*, 80.

metamorphosis. From desired to damned, from loved to feared, it revels in its comedies and tragedies, its scandals and triumphs.

It is a key that is difficult to fit to the art of acting. In the artistic code of the theater, in contrast to our usual understanding, repetition does not mean always the same. You cannot duplicate a production. Acting in the theater is not a technical reproduction that can be played at the press of a button. It is not always the same film, even if the same play is produced and the same text is spoken. A production is not a closed circle, and actors do not clone themselves. That would quickly be boring. The play would have no air to breathe, the greatest effort would be for nothing, the words would not grow wings; rather, they would stick to the paper they were written on, remain dead, morphemic corpses. The plot would plod, a merely theoretical vessel. You might as well buy the theater program and just read it instead. A "mechanical" repetition squanders the most beautiful and difficult aspect of theater: the possibility it holds of eventfulness. In doing so it cheats the audience of live observation, which is probably, in our media-saturated world, what still draws people to the theater; assuming they are not satisfied with mere representation on stage and in the auditorium, but that their pleasure in theater is drawn from the endless openness of everything that lives.

Yet again, once more, one more time for the umpteenth time. These words also have a whiff of coercion and of compulsion that robs us of our freedom when they emerge all powerful from our subconscious. But theater has nothing to do with this, even if actors are sometimes plagued by a theatrical superego in the form of directors, managers, and critics. Unlike compulsive repetition, an actor's repetition is joyful, happy. It is not beyond, but within the pleasure principle.[50] It is the pleasurable site of creativity, the pool of regeneration.

Why?

Each performance is a repetition of the performance before it. Either way. Whatever it was, it was. When the lights go down, the curtain falls, the actors have taken their bow and returned to their dressing rooms, and the audience has gone to get their coats; the performance is over,

---

50 "But we come now to a new and remarkable fact, namely that the compulsion to repeat also recalls from the past experiences which include no possibility of pleasure." Sigmund Freud, *Beyond the Pleasure Principle*, trans. James Strachey. *The Standard Edition of the Complete Psychological Works of Sigmund Freud*, vol. 18. (London: The Hogarth Press, 1971), 20.

finished, completed. But, and this is what's fantastic about theater, on the next night, the next performance date, it can be repeated and new life can be breathed into it at each repetition. It can be repotentialized. What does that mean? Each individual performance is saved in the actor's memory as a result of the rehearsal process – all directions, all the right and wrong turns, thoughts, feelings, texts, contexts, appearances, entrances, exits – the entire fabric of scenes and dialogues. They have been inscribed within him and memorized. He can draw from them and play them again and again, and each performance lays down another memory pathway, so that his archive continually becomes fuller and richer. But only if the actor risks what has been before and frees it can he again electrify it. Only if he time and again and once more risks opening his acting to the uncertainty of his movements does a performance take off. This act of creative repetition is what makes acting so electrifying. It is its aesthetic desire, for the actors and for the audience. It opens all involved to a temporal piece of art that defies common sense, the reason of the everyday. Or perhaps it opens them to the gift of the muses that allows the dawning of an era in which the law of chronology no longer holds. The actor looks to the remembered past. He brings it into the present word for word, situation for situation and at the same time sends it into the future word for word, situation for situation by taking all that has happened and again exposing it to the openness of the present. In this way, he secures the future of his acting. There is no closure, because it is reopened in every performance. The actor may be chained to the chronology of the plot and to a certain setting, but in the kairos of time – in the present, past, and future – he can again find, recognize, develop, and remember new and ever more complex meanings in the play and its performative form. He can make good on something he maybe owes the play. He can go back to what has been in time and make up for lapses after the fact.

For this reason the difference in each repeated performance is always also an act of freedom and of liberation, an act of regeneration.[51] He overturns the past and present because the future acts within him – always unique, always singular. For this reason it is not the same performance that is given each evening in each show with the same name, but each

---

51 Arno Böhler, "Nietzsche – Vom regenerativen Charakter des Gemüts," *psycho-logik 2, Existenz und Gefühl* (2007).

performance keeps its initial character and each repetition is bound to transgress the boundary of what has once been this way or that. This is the struggle or favor of theater in the actor's art of repetition. His acting in the present must always be coupled to what has been and what will be, whether he succeeds or fails.

Discovering and reviving the gap inherent to the future breathes new life into *the act* of all action, all emotions, all thoughts, and all speech. Without this difference[52] it is impotent, and it has no animating aura. Only if the play is performed from the very gut of the actor's archive, only if it is played as if it has just been discovered and spoken for the first time do the actions within it acquire meaning – even that which cannot be explained and remains mysterious. Without this difference and without the corporeal commitment to this difference, the actor would be nothing but a marionette whose mechanics could at most be hidden by the telescope of representation.[53]

By initializing and preserving this immanent difference in every repetition, the actor repotentializes his performance.[54] It becomes pneumatic. This is how he can escape the drudgery of doing one and the same thing each night and breathe new life into the play without it remaining one and the same, and also without willfully breaking with the performance that was worked upon and that the company agreed upon. In *triggering difference*, a play and its text begin to live, to speak; they begin to speak to the audience. The words take on physicality. They develop intensity as a material quality. They are charged and penetrate hearts, loins, and minds to spin their sensuous net of meanings and connections. Each word is just the tip of an iceberg. All actions are only what is visible of much more complex interconnections that reach into what is absent, missing, and incongruous.

Such a flowing repetition, and that which can be seen in it, can get you hooked, can hang its barbs onto the most inaccessible reaches of your subconscious.

Is this art not yet another reason to want to become an actor?

---

52 For a concept of thought that matches this, see Gilles Deleuze, *Difference and Repetition*, trans. Paul Patton (New York: Athlone Press, 1994).
53 Hoffmann, *The Sandman*.
54 Böhler, *Singularitäten*, 165–183.

The Gift of Acting 97

Figure 6.1 One of eight Dionysus masks made for the chorus in the lecture performance *Nach(t) der Tragödie* (After/The Night of the Tragedy). Courtesy of GRENZ_film, böhler&granzer, 2010. Mask designed and created by Elisabeth Binder-Neurue.

Heiner Müller: I am a land surveyor

One could say that the basic element of theater, and of drama too, is transformation, and that death is the last transformation. The only thing common to everyone in the audience, that can make an audience one, is the fear of death, everyone has it ... and the effect of theater rests on this only commonality. The foundation of theater is therefore always a symbolic death.[55]

---

55 Alexander Kluge and Heiner Müller, *Ich bin ein Landvermesser*, 176.

Jean Paul: First Flower-Piece

Frozen, dumb nothingness! Cold, eternal necessity! [...] How lonely is everyone in the wide charnel of the universe! [...] Alas! If every being is its own father and creator, why cannot it also be its own destroying angel? [...] Look down into the abyss over which clouds of ashes are floating by. Fogs full of worlds arise out of the sea of death. The future is a rising vapour, the present a falling one. [...] And after death [...] when the man of sorrows stretches his sore wounded back upon the earth to slumber towards a lovelier morning [...] no morning cometh.[56]

---

56 Jean Paul, *Flower, Fruit and Thorn-Pieces*, trans. Alexander Ewing (London: George Bell, 1892), 280–281.

Except where otherwise noted, this work is licensed under a Creative Commons Attribution 4.0 International License. To view a copy of this license, visit https://creativecommons.org/version4

OPEN

7
The Gift of Death

Abstract: *Here we begin to delve into the true heart of the art of acting. If theater is no longer understood as a theater of representation, then what takes place on stage is a transformation at play with truth. Heiner Müller called it a symbolic death, the most central event of the theater. Its most fundamental and most intimate impact stems from the fear, shared by audience and actors, of the caesura of death and the horror of the definitive loss of ourselves as subjects.*

But does the fascination of theater not draw from the pleasure of metamorphosis, from gain, surplus, and the joy of the singular rightness of conditions? This interpretation ends in an ethical expectation of theater in which the stage becomes a site that reminds us what we, qua our existence, might have become. Such a foolish fable of felicitousness seems anachronistic. But the time of theater is outside of our time, it is a time of promises.

Valerie, Susanne. *Actors and the Art of Performance: Under Exposure.* Basingstoke: Palgrave Macmillan, 2016. DOI: 10.1057/9781137596345.0013.

Tu es mort

Death is none of our business, because as long as we are, death is not and when death is, we are no longer, as Epicurus noted more than two thousand years ago.

But *your* death is my business. *You* are dead. Now I will never ever see you again. This is the only reason I know what dying, what death, means. Only *your* death reveals to me the radical nature of death. *Your* death renders me inconsolable. Tears a hole in my life.

The first death is the death of the other, not our own. It is the only reason we know that we are mortal.

Our hearts torn open, time torn open. A fissure, a gap and abyss into which past, present, and future disappear. The time of death sucks them in, obliterated, nothing left but emptiness. When it opens its eyelids without lashes, there are no eyes behind them, only black ugly caves.

The clock face of eternity on which no number is written and which is its own hand. A horrible black finger pointing to an empty dial – for the dead want to see their time on it, Jean Paul says.

Ananke turns *kairos* into its opposite.

No longer a propitious moment, the fate of necessity, which also brings death, has irrevocably, irreversibly taken you from me and with you pulled everything into absence. "Sum in puncto desperationis," wrote Friedrich Nietzsche to Franz Overbeck in 1881. Desperation as standstill, a full stop.

Theater as a symbolic death

The time has come, in this research on the actor, to return to the beginning: The case of drama student Hannah J. in auditorium X.

The search engine that began combing for answers to what had happened has meanwhile filled many pages with ideas. It crashed and was rebooted many times, and many trial runs were carried out. Its hits were all over the place: aspects, splinters, fragmentary observations, impressions, theses, speculations, and descriptions of phenomena. Whether directly or indirectly, they also always pointed back to Hannah J.

Paradoxically, contrary to all "reasonable" expectations, Hannah J. broke into tears and stopped playing just at the moment when her acting became creative. She refused to act any further and was overcome with a sudden aversion to becoming an actor, although it had been her most coveted desire.

Her audience tried to understand why. Why did she stop? What blow was she dealt? What trap door opened? Was Hannah J. crying for herself? Was she rebelling against the event of a symbolic death? Did she stare directly into the contemporary mask of Dionysus,[1] which masks nothingness, the caesura of death inherent to the heart of all creativity? Did the shock of the absence behind the mask, the fear of being abandoned and left to the bottomless stage of our being-in-the-world threaten her subliminal image of the world and of the sovereignty of the subject? Did the act of engaging acting attack this common sense and transform it into "holy earnest,"[2] so that instead of joy the young actor was overcome by the deathly fear identified by Heiner Müller? The siren song of a monster in the actor's art of metamorphosis. But it was not a "harmless"

---

1 Walter Otto, "The Symbol of the Mask," in *Dionysus Myth and Cult*, 86–92.
2 Huizinga, 23.

A closed metal top, a second wooden cover, the trace of your face gone, no longer to be gazed upon. The thought of the cold storage box into which the dead are pushed in our culture makes my desperation even greater. Everything has been obliterated with you, fallen into a coma. Time does not pass or last, kairos and chronos have both been paralyzed, destroyed. Hermetically sealed, being is only misery. Everything drags, listless, lustless, apathetic, hopeless, and pointless, and fear has a field day. It is a diffuse insubordinate fear that gets in everywhere. Fear's shadow is on the walls, the ceiling, the air, in each and every breath. The present is only a never again. The future is only a never again. The past is only the pain of never again. Time is only lack. Holding on in vain. Everything is unapproachable, inaccessible, remote. Life is swallowed up by its absence. *You are no longer here* destroys everything else.

The extreme absence conjured by your death eggs fear on, day by day, night by night, uncanny and all powerful. Especially mornings. Fear lies heavy as a coffin lid on my breast. It is insistent that one day there will really be no more mornings, no future, no place to hide. One day, everything will truly be destroyed forever by death and, the unwelcome appendix, we can fail completely, our end can be nothing more than a dead end. We might not notice until it is too late, while dying, expiring under an indifferent sky. Cursed, abandoned, lost, and finally forgotten, because there is no time in which there could have been a happy ending. False deceptive words, the useless comfort of a childish desire.

transformation such as we usually understand it, one that takes place in the narrative, but a central element in the event of the play, from which the familiar ego is not sure it will emerge unscathed. Cunning Odysseus had his companions, their ears closed with wax, tie him to the mast so that he could enjoy the siren's song without plunging to his death. Did Hannah J. quickly close all her senses because, cut loose, she felt the unfamiliar, frightening pull of the exposure of her very own existence? Was her stubborn self-censure of theater an emergency brake so that she would not be tempted to wander any further into dangerous territory? "The psyche's extended: knows nothing about it," Freud wrote on August 22, 1938, in a note published posthumously, a note the philosopher Jean-Luc Nancy called Freud's "most fascinating and ... perhaps most decisive statement."[3]

Perhaps something similar happened in auditorium X. Perhaps it was the event of suddenly experiencing the strange extension of the psyche beyond her own skin – but how far? where to? Or perhaps the intimidating experience of, so to speak, losing herself in play, which blew apart the fictional aspect of theater. Yes, maybe that is how it was. There is no other reason to break into tears at the moment when everything falls into place, no other reason to swear off theater. This irritation obviously got under her skin; it hurt her, it was emotional, full of pathos, a real acid test.

---

3 Jean-Luc Nancy, *Corpus*, 21.

Where is Paul Celan's counterword, the word that cuts the string, the step taken toward freedom? Sure, in art, anything can happen in art. But what about in real life? Without a stage, without a theater, without a prompter, without a text committed to memory? There is no word there, no counterword. There is only emptiness of heart and mind, only complete absence. Meaninglessness, greedy as cancer, begins to spread and takes over strength, joy, happiness, and perception in general until an eyeless, mouthless mask has grown over one's own face.

Without a gaze, being loses its orientation, runs around in circles. Round and round. A circle that continually runs into the same dead end of powerlessness, a circle of depression, of fear, a vicious circle – and the devil laughs up his sleeve.

Which specter is haunting here?
"Where wilt thou lead me? speak, I'll go no further."[4]

back at the same place fallen into the same trap where language fails where grammar dissolves and the sudden shock remains a fear that will not be shaken immune to reason ethereal reflections cut off from torn away from myself forced into absence although we actors are all about presence can always only be present the principle of my individuation has been violated gambled away disclosed exposed

absence in simultaneous presence destabilizing paradox how can i find words for a vacuum at the center of my being words that unburden explain enlighten when they have moved to the sphere of the unsayable outside exscribing as i read in corpus without understanding what it means jesus mary and joseph my grandfather would now bellow this confounded hole the actor disappears into without disappearing this pitfall of play this almost point of no return what kind of game is that you can play with-out me count me out

Point of no return

At the point of no return there is no stopping, and free will is lamed. The turn is a tear in time, a caesura where something happens that cannot be undone. Something comes to an end. A border is crossed, a blow dealt – and the result is a transformation, either of one's outer form or of one's relation to oneself. Either way, afterward nothing is as it was before. Many a text discusses this phenomenon.

For example, the Joan of Arc monologue that Hannah J. was struggling with in auditorium X mentions two turning points before which Joan stood helplessly. In the first, the shepherdess is called by God to liberate France, and in the second she is in battle with the English General Lionel. That time the turn is caused by looking into the eyes of a man. It is a gaze of love that enters her and makes it impossible for her to kill the enemy as she has killed others before him, although she has won. "My heart is changed with many alterings," she cries, bemoaning this gaze, which also silences the voice of God within her.[5]

---

4 William Shakespeare, *Hamlet*, in *The Illustrated Stratford Shakespeare*, 804; on this see also Jacques Derrida, *Specters of Marx*, 21.

5 Friedrich Schiller, *The Maid of Orleans*, 86.

A scandalous contradiction is raised here.

In the era of Weimar classicism, Friedrich Schiller found a "moral" answer to Joan's point of no return. On the one hand, there is her death in battle. How could she, guiltlessly guilty, go on living? Joan has to die; she must forfeit her life in battle. On the other hand, this death is made meaningful by her posthumous elevation to sainthood.

On the battlefield of the stage, the actor is exposed to a similarly offensive contradiction and is paradoxically simultaneously guilty and innocent because he is caught between power and powerlessness, or passivity and action, or being with and with-out himself. When this differentiation occurs in him, his acting loses its naiveté or, to borrow from Johan Huizinga, it loses its profane, everyday character. This realization does not take place on an intellectual level. Rather, it stems from the corporeal experience of being simultaneously appropriated and expropriated while acting. All at once the actor *knows* that for the rest of his life he must abandon himself to this process. One might call the effects *differentiations* or *wounds* that tear open one's very existence, the fragility of the unforeseeable.[6] Its secret. Or you could call these effects the absent, the elusive, that which remains unsolved. The ego-alien, the dark Other of our selves, that which the ego is unable to tame and can never be predicted, no matter what the event.

This can, of course, disturb someone deeply, as it must have Hannah J., and suddenly and completely change the feelings they used to have about theater. Suddenly acting is no longer non-committal, and the play loses the protective veneer of mere representation behind which the actor, consciously or unconsciously, can hide, behind which he can, in the end, keep Heiner Müller's idea about theatrical transformation at bay.

But which law dictates that fear is the only ruler of transformation? Why should fear alone join actor and audience so powerfully – only the threat of future loss and no gain?

Against Müller, we can insist that joy and wanton desire are also able to burst upon actor and audience and exert the same magical draw. The ancient emblem of the theater is twofold. The mourning of tragedy is linked to the pleasure of comedy. At the end the beginning is waiting.

---

6   Compare Jean-Luc Nancy, *Corpus*.

Even in its fictive preemption. Doesn't anticipation pervade all of reality, anticipation of possibilities that preempt themselves?

But when the ability to differentiate has been awakened, what might the liberating blow look like that catapults us into joy and opens the possibility that the jumping jack need not remain a marionette tangled in its strings, lying knotted and lifeless in the corner? Does abandoning our self hold a promise that we can read in the example of the actor?

The meanings of abandon[7] range from renounce, desert, disown, jilt, reject to abandoning ship, leaving to die. With its connotations of being left, discarded, washing hands of, it is a threatening word. But it has another meaning – uninhibited surrender – which adds a more positive twist.

Etymologically, abandon stems from the French *à bandon*, at the discretion of, a legal term used in the 3rd century when forests were opened for anyone to freely cut down wood – hence the sense of giving up control, letting go, a gift.

These dual meanings follow us from the celebratory fearful moment of our birth through life and finally death. Thus seen, the need to abandon oneself – the "symbolic death" in the transformation of theater – is not necessarily synonymous with desertion and destruction.

We could flip the whole thing around!

Felicity – a salto mortale

The "true world" finally became a fable, it was said.

So why shouldn't we spin fables about more than fear and death, with its modern insistence on the precedence of total impermanence. Doesn't the modern panacea of economic growth also speculate shamelessly, amidst the finite and despite all finality, even if it goes against all reason?[8] Besides, this is theater after all, where there is always conflict about who gets which role, especially the lead. So why should we leave the stage to the Grim Reaper in the role of the last remaining god?

---

7 *Preisgeben* in the German original, a word that stems from *preisen*, to praise and *geben*, to give – trans.

8 Fred Luks, *Endlich im Endlichen. Oder: Warum die Rettung der Welt Ironie und Großzügigkeit erfordert* (Marburg: Metropolis, 2010).

"From hour to hour, we ripe and ripe, / And then, from hour to hour, we rot and rot, / And thereby hangs a tale,"[9] as the Shakespearean fool Touchstone says.

Certainly.

But which tale? The tale of the last legitimate European self-certitude about puppets on a string that does not break because it is programmed to move inexorably toward death, while we (stinginess is sexy! as a popular German ad campaign proclaims) try to console ourselves with golden coins? Why shouldn't we spin fables that go beyond this last myth of European modernity,[10] without automatically being stigmatized as trying to take refuge in a backward world? Why shouldn't we, without automatically choosing the opposite path, hear the crow of the rooster not only as the call to nihilism but *also* as a call to a future beautiful morning?

Would it set off too many idiosyncrasies?

We are so forgiving of fools of the theater. Why not give them some credit?

But everyone is on credit. There is nothing left to give. We only believe in the dark fatality of our being. Even if we try to repress, ignore, or be indifferent to the sirens' song, it has its effect, "and wide around lie human bones that whiten all the ground."[11]

What have we humans done in some black chasm of the black sky that we were given the punishment of living?

As if in retribution for some unknown disgraceful deed, we are torn from a shapeless, painless, nameless peace and herded into kicking, gnawing bodies that, driven by their hunger and their thirst, by their hate, their fear or just their complete stupidity, will still end up mutilated on some battlefield of life. And even if we succeed in becoming old and frail [...] in the end we finally also perish at the decree of some merciless creator – from our hunger for life, our destructive urges or just the simple progression of time.[12]

---

9   William Shakespeare, *As You Like It*, Act II Scene VII, 223.
10 Hans-Dieter Bahr, *Den Tod denken* (Munich: Fink, 2002), 10.
11 Homer, The Odyssey, trans. Alexander Pope (South Bend: Ex Fontibus, 2012), 206.
12 Christoph Ransmayr, *Odysseus, Verbrecher. Schauspiel einer Heimkehr* (Frankfurt am Main: Fischer, 2010), 11.

Thus begins Christoph Ransmayr's version of the return of Odysseus after the destruction of Troy. *Odysseus Verbrecher* (outlaw) is now the name of the hero of Homer's epic poem, one of the milestones of the beginnings of Western culture. It is a grand nihilistic excess similar to Jean Paul's *Speech of the Dead Christ*, with the difference that this *Schauspiel einer Heimkehr* (Homecoming drama) reads like a tragic, late modern era echo of the sirens' song. There is no longer a nightmare vision of the future. The 20th century has drowned itself in blood, and the tragedies of annihilation continue – wearing many masks – with no end in sight.

Slaughter and murder is a caesura with no homecoming. Odysseus the "destroyer of cities" returns, but he has become another, and the long period of waiting has also irreversibly changed Penelope. No reparations can be made. It is no longer possible for them to embrace. Their past love, their old happiness has rotted away, lost and betrayed. Neither has their son Telemachus been spared. Traumatically, he is pulled into a new cycle of killing and dying.

Homo sacer, accursed man, who knows no refuge from death.[13] Homo sacer, holy man, holder of the *lumen naturale*, the light of knowledge. Ill-fated equivocality that allows him to understand the beauty and horror that permeate the world.

"'It is ten o'clock:
Thus we may see,' quoth he, 'how the world wags:
'Tis but an hour ago since it was nine,
And after one hour more 'twill be eleven;
And so, from hour to hour, we ripe and ripe,
And then, from hour to hour, we rot and rot;
And thereby hangs a tale.' When I did hear
The motley fool thus moral on the time,
My lungs began to crow like chanticleer.
That fools should be so deep-contemplative,
And I did laugh sans intermission
An hour by his dial."[14]

---

13 Giorgio Agamben, *Homo* Sacer, trans. Daniel Heller-Roazen (Stanford: Stanford University Press, 2011).
14 William Shakespeare, *As You Like It*, Act II Scene VII, 223.

If in *As You Like It* William Shakespeare's melancholy figure Jacques is right – who cannot stop laughing about Touchstone the fool's reasoning – then the stages of this world and the theater performed upon them are nothing but a space on which we can die of laughter upon hearing the profound memento mori spoken by motley fools.

And crossing this stage of the world, following Müller's gaze *Under the Sign of Saturn*,[15] the theater is only a space where we remember ourselves as someone who might die, joined only in our fear of death, the final horizon.

Why not? Who says it is not so?

Fortune. Felicity.

The fabulous occurrence of a rapturous performance.

Another reason to die laughing?

As you like it.

The incorrigibility of fortune is controversial. As it should be. In the flitting comedy of errors that is the fable of truth, each must find out for themselves where they belong. No one is spared from slipping up.

When a performance really hits the mark, a sort of side jump occurs, an unexpected turn, a peripeteia that no reasoning can touch. If someone says it was only a chimera, you will feel stupid, ashamed, liable to stutter like a fool. There is no conclusive explanation for felicity, only attempts to describe the event and its effects. Reflection cannot define it definitively; it is against the reign of ideas that assumes all concepts can be delimited and fixed in all their interrelations. Delineation and adjudication reach their limits at felicity. It opens a flowing current, a soma current, an overflow that robs both the occidental white narcotic[16] of objective science as well as the sirens' song of its power. Interconnections abound and become fruitful. Lush, voluptuous, oriental. They are extravagant and generous. Their coupling, the coupling of the muses, a constant *copula*, is continuously creative. The gap created by the leap to the side, the escapade, by breaking the rules and norms, lets something in which had previously been barred. The blind spot becomes a pore that sees without seeing and opens itself, replicates itself playfully, again and again. A new pore, another space for something new is created. There is no end.

---

15 Susan Sontag, *Under the Sign of Saturn* (New York: Farrar, Straus and Giroux: 1980).

16 Jacques Derrida, "White Mythology. Metaphor in the Text of Philosophy" in *New Literary History*, vol. 6(1), (August 1974): 5–74.

Perhaps we could say that the foundation of felicity is porosity. The fruitful, fertile, fecund openings with which felicity shares its root, felix. It is sited outside of our ability to reason logically, outside the logical concept of understanding and within the realm of the metaphor, the trope, the fable, and the disposition that does not deny but welcomes knowledge.

In the pathos of a propitious performance we understand that although death ends life, it does not undo birth; that the impossible is possible and yet the possible still impossible; that everything is transformed even though nothing has changed. Its potency suspends the irrevocability of the past. The structure of polar opposites is suspended in favor of another, altered state in which attentiveness and generosity reign and protect against the poison of ressentiment, even overriding its reactionary system – at least for a moment. The ear behind your ear opens, the eye behind your eye, with passion in reason and reason in passion, your heart in your mouth and your mouth in your heart. They all become transparent to each other, wink at each other conspiratorially. They are players in the same game the aim of which is not to attain the highest number, but to have everything be as right as it can be. In accomplishment and in joy the taste of all the senses tickles the palate. The smell of rot and decay has vanished, and the apple we bite into is not poisoned.

Our friend Touchstone

Basking in the forest sun, Shakespeare's fool Touchstone argues with Lady Fortune about her moodiness. And even when he speaks foolishly, he does so wisely, but in vain. There is no sense in logical argumentation with that lady. You need to give that up, he says. Therefore he may not be called a fool until destiny, the lucky break, happiness has fallen upon him from heaven, when Lady Fortune's wheel has turned to his advantage and her cornucopia is poured upon him. "Call me not fool till heaven hath sent me fortune."[17] An ironic play with words, a keen insight, a silly aberration? How should we understand what Touchstone says?

---

17 Shakespeare, *As You Like It*, Act 2, Scene 7, 223.

Perhaps his contradictory back and forth – "a motley fool, a miserable world"[18] – is meant to put the riddle of Fortuna, of luck, to the touchstone and determine its measure of gold.

Thus perhaps his name.

In Shakespeare's time, a touchstone was originally used to determine the measure of gold in a stone. A sample was rubbed on a touchstone until it left a visible line, the color of which was compared to pure gold. Touchstone's name can, of course, be understood metaphorically. The fool rubs his thoughts against the riddle of fortune to determine not whether it is gold, the possession of which is said to make the world go around, but another glittering treasure. Touchstone is looking for the gleam, the shine, the aura of fortune, the person luck has shone upon and who, full of joy, himself shines.

The art of the actor can be an example of this. When acting is fortunate and talent and accomplishment are kissed by the muses in a propitious moment, the actors emanate a particular gleam, a shining, a certain aura. This aura is more than their mimetic art and cannot be reduced to an aesthetic grammar. It should not be confused with the aura of a fascinating or charismatic person. The luminescence of felicity is not the potentiation of the subject who captivates through the power of his talent and his personality alone. Rather, it is a sign of the limits of the power of the subject, its crisis. The coercive experience of an Other takes place within the aura of fortune or felicitous play; it provokes a transformation of the ego or, in Müller's words, its "symbolic death." The auratic element of on-stage transformation marks, if you will, the much talked-about death of the subject, which is suddenly no longer the source and foundation of knowledge, freedom, speech, and history, and paradoxically at the same time regains itself as *subiectum*. *Its* aura is the numinosity of the "unique apparition of a distance, however near it may be."[19]

---

18 Ibid.

19 Walter Benjamin, *The Work of Art in the Age of Its Technological Reproducibility*, trans. by Michel W. Jennings (Cambridge: Belknap Press, 2008), 23.

What to do? In the middle of playing in fortune's favor, to be – *quel malheur!* – unexpectedly waylaid by fear like Hannah J. and then recoil? How could she suddenly do what she could not do before and what price did she pay?

Or – *quel bonheur!* – to be waylaid by joy and give yourself over to the passion of this turn, this moment of *kairos*, a *salto mortale* that went well, which in this risky game can mean returning to itself? This does not mean giving up your freedom but willingly surrendering to a look of love in the eyes of being. An affirmative, consensual look. A look of resignation, giving oneself up without fear because a look of love is always a yes and not a no. Because it is both pledge and promise of trust and generosity rather than of lack and loss.

Theater champions a great diversity of concepts, needs, desires, ideas, and paradigms.

But if an actor is electrified by the autopoetic power of theatrical art, then the art of the actor is not only the virtuosity of his ability. Neither is it the representation of factual reality, that is to say, the reproduction of what is already there and known, no matter how much mimetic pleasure this can give both actor and audience. Neither does it have to do solely with political or ideological content. The electrostatic[20] thread of Ariadne in the art of acting, no matter what the aesthetic form, is in carrying the monstrosity of our existence, the corporeal creative path *from the self to the self*. Inward and outward, the trapdoor of an always unique event. Extreme exposition leads to extreme intimacy, and extreme intimacy leads to extreme exposition – always in the state of being with each other. The uncanny transforms enthusiastically into astonishment about how we can transcend our own possibilities, go beyond our own subjectivity, while still only showing this with ourselves and through ourselves. *With-out me* transforms from horror to joy about the never-ending difference in that which is spoken and promised together, that which we, here and now, might once become. Theater as a chamber of the sublime could be the common space of re-membering the potentiality of human existence.

---

20 "*Elektra* means 'the shining sun.' A gold-silver alloy is known as *electrum*, which in turn comes from amber, *electron* the root of our *electricity*." Elisabeth von Samsonow, *Anti-Elektra* (Zurich: diaphanes, 2007), 9.

The event of the performative in the acting process is made up, as we have seen, of the conscious absorption of a critical reworking of one's own archive, the historical and the personal archive. The responsibility and the ethos of the actor must be to embrace this pathos, this passion, this *passio* – to be its physiological witness. He owes this to his talent, to promise himself to that which is existential within repetition, as a category of the future, a possibility that is always becoming, not as a promise of a tomorrow that never comes, but of one that can, and does indeed, arrive in the moment of a felicitous, providential performance.

Against the spirit of our epoch, it might be time to reinstate beauty, felicity, and fortune in the canon of art.

L'avenir du bonheur! L'avenir de la beauté!

Except where otherwise noted, this work is licensed under a Creative Commons Attribution 4.0 International License. To view a copy of this license, visit https://creativecommons.org/version4

OPEN

8
Finale and Punctum

Abstract: *A fabulous promise.*
Why do you want to be an actor?

Valerie, Susanne. *Actors and the Art of Performance: Under Exposure.* Basingstoke: Palgrave Macmillan, 2016.
DOI: 10.1057/9781137596345.0014.

Why do you want to be an actor?

For many very different reasons. But also and more than anything for this reason:

Why should we pay homage to the marionette lying broken in the corner? A dead puppet with a cold heart. But why shouldn't it, just for fun, take an extra skip, a jump in the air, a jump for joy, and thumb his nose at nihilism? Transformed into a fool, he basks in the sun in a forest clearing and, whispering, memorizes the fable of *amor fati*, which is to open soon.

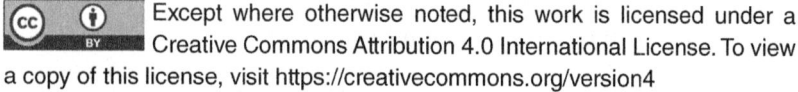 Except where otherwise noted, this work is licensed under a Creative Commons Attribution 4.0 International License. To view a copy of this license, visit https://creativecommons.org/version4

The manufacturer's authorised representative in the EU is Springer Nature Customer Service Centre GmbH, Europaplatz 3, 69115 Heidelberg, Germany. If you have any concerns regarding our products, please contact ProductSafety@springernature.com

Printed and bound by CPI Group (UK) Ltd, Croydon, CR0 4YY
23/03/2026
02076443-0002